101 Thoughts for a Better Life

101 Thoughts for a Better Life

Steve Feazel

VW

Vision Word

www.visionword.com

Vision Word - Gambier, Ohio

All rights reserved. No part of this book may be reproduced or transmitted in any form or by any means without written permission of the author.

All scripture quotations, unless otherwise noted, taken from THE HOLY BIBLE, NEW INTERBATIONAL VERSION, NIV Copyright © 1973, 1978, 1984, 2011 by Biblica, Inc. Used by permission. All rights reserved worldwide

ISBN 9798871667354

Cover Design: Steve Feazel

Cover Photo: Gary Alvis

Dedication

To the memory of my grandmother, Dulcy Feazel, who first directed my family to a faith in Jesus Christ.

Acknowledgments

Much gratitude is extended to my editors: my wife Edy, and our friend Amy Fovargue. I am thankful for my friends at my Tuesday morning Bible Study who have provided inspiring encouragement for this project.

Introduction

We are where our decisions take us and decisions are made from thoughts that we focus on in our minds. Paul said in Romans 12:2: Do not conform to the pattern of this world, but be transformed by the renewing of your mind. Then you will be able to test and approve what God's will is—his good, pleasing and perfect will. The Apostle Paul realized that the way you think and what you think about will affect the quality of your life. He revealed that thinking in the pattern of this world does not render positive results. A Christian is to have a mind renewed by Jesus Christ.

Paul provided more on this topic in Philippians 4:8: "Finally, brothers and sisters, whatever is true, whatever is noble, whatever is right, whatever is pure, whatever is lovely, whatever is admirable—if anything is excellent or praiseworthy—think about such things." Paul gives a list of the categories that will enhance the activity of our minds in this verse. Basically, if you think about the wrong things, you will end up doing the wrong things. We are all familiar with the saying, "Garbage in, garbage out." It is commonly applied to some computer program, but it is also very applicable to our minds.

The British writer, James Allen, who was active in the late 1800s and early 1900s, wrote a small book entitled, *As a Man Thinketh*, in 1902. He took the title from Proverbs 23:7: "For as he thinks in his heart, so is he" (NKJV). There is a great deal of truth in this proverb which conveys that the character we display to the world was first forged in the thinking we allowed to go on in our mind. Allen's words agree, "A noble character is not a thing of favor or chance, but the natural result of continued effort in right thinking, the effect of long-cherished association with noble thoughts." (*As a Man Thinketh* p. 16)

Allen and the Apostle Paul stand in total agreement with each other when it comes to our thinking. They reveal when one comes to Jesus Christ he or she must give the Lord their mind as well as their heart. I enjoy the mystery crime stories of Hercule Poirot created by Agatha Christie, which have appeared in books, on television and in film. This Belgian detective who practices his craft in England is always referring to his "little gray cells" as his number one asset in solving a case. We are in need of our little gray cells thinking on things that are in harmony with the principles of our Christian faith and not harboring thoughts promoted by the world. James 1:14-15 states: $_{14}$ "but each person is tempted when they are dragged away by their own evil desire and enticed. $_{15}$ Then, after desire has conceived, it gives birth to sin; and sin, when it is full-grown, gives birth to death."

The dragging away takes place in your mind. That's where Satan gets a foothold when he brings temptation. It is a downward spiral from that point on if you welcome the temptation. There is desire that leads to enticement that leads to sin and then sin to death. It is not a good ending and it all begins in the mind. This book is written to help the reader embrace noble thoughts that will lead to good thinking that will produce a better Christian character.

There are no chapters in this book, only a numbered list of thoughts with brief comments by the author on each thought enhancing its truth. Hopefully some of these thoughts will have a powerful impact on the reader's life. The various thoughts are the author's own, noted by his initials, "SF." Some others are Scripture verses, quotes from famous people of history, and common sayings. The format is simplistic and the content easily understood. God often uses the simple and the ordinary to generate awesome deeds.

James Allen penned wise words when he wrote, "A man's mind is like a garden, which may be intelligently cultivated or allowed to run wild. But cultivated or neglected it must, and will bring forth." (As a Man Thinketh p. 21) I am hopeful that the reader will find the thoughts in this book to be good and useful seeds resulting in a beautiful harvest of a better life.

Steve Teazel

Thoughts

1. In the school of life, the classroom is Time and Experience is the teacher. Learn your lessons well. – SF

The first time I spoke this line in public was at the high school graduation ceremony of the home school students in my local county. Hopefully, some of them might have remembered this line at least for a few weeks, as they embarked on their next chapter in life. The truth in these words is obvious, but it is not always followed. Some do not learn their lessons well and pay a detrimental price as a consequence.

We all learn from experience and adjust to life accordingly. A baby learns that its cry brings milk. The restaurant where food is bland and the service is poor will lose customers. Working your job overtime gives you experience that makes you perform better, and your skills improve. We all prefer a surgeon with experience and the same for our pilot. In the work place, time provides the experience which allows you to measure people. You learn with whom it is best to share new ideas and whom to avoid interacting with, because their attitude or values don't align well with yours.

This thought at the top of the page is a reality, constantly in play in every aspect of living including your spiritual life. Sometimes in the mundane things of life the lessons are not learned well as Teacher Experience is ignored. The overeating that caused indigestion is repeated. Choosing fun over preparing for the test, when repeated, still results in a poor grade. When experience teaches you lessons in the spiritual realm and they are not learned, your soul suffers.

The children of Israel experienced a number of miracles in their exodus from Egypt. The Passover which spared them the death of their first born and their walk on the dry path through the sea were two incredible ones, but when Moses was a long time on top of the mountain, they chose to worship a golden calf they created. The disciples of Jesus saw the healing miracles, the feeding of the multitudes and the raising of Lazarus, but they scattered in fear when their Lord was arrested and crucified.

Many Christians today have fared no better than these biblical examples of failure in spiritual faithfulness. They received salvation when they repented of their sins and were thrilled in the joy experienced. They had times when God answered a prayer for a daunting problem they faced and times when he showered them with blessings, but these experiences were not remembered when temptation came and they yielded to it. They did not learn well from the teacher of experience in the spiritual classroom and their fellowship with their Lord was broken as self replaced Jesus in their hearts. Has this ever happened to you? If it has, you have a forgiving Lord who wants you back. Ask for his forgiveness and restore your walk with him. The Bible says: "If we confess our sins, he is faithful and just and will forgive us our sins and purify us from all unrighteousness." (1 John 1:9)

Some people do repeat the same mistake. Maybe they hope for a different result or maybe they lack the wisdom to learn from experience. One thing is for certain, if you do not learn your spiritual lessons well from experience, it will be eternally damaging.

2. The past is unchangeable. The present is a moment where you can do something to make the future better. – SF

You can't change history. People may try to rewrite it, but that still does not change it. History is everything in the past up to the present moment. The present is in constant motion into the future, which means that history is constantly expanding. I have more history related to my life today than I did yesterday, and I can't change any of it. The same is true for you. You may look on the past with regret, wishing you had made different decisions, but there is nothing you can do to change the past.

You can, however, do the right thing in the present that will create positive results in the future. This will help you create a better history, as time passes, as well as a better future. This is true in your work life and your family life, but more importantly it is true in your spiritual life. You may have a past filled with shameful sins. You can't change it, but the good news is in Jesus Christ you can have total forgiveness in a present moment as you repent of your sins and have a new future set before you that will include eternal life in heaven. Paul writes in 2 Corinthians 5:17: "Therefore, if anyone is in Christ, the new creation has come. The old has gone, the new is here!"

Jesus told Nicodemus that he must be born again. Jesus of course, meant this in a spiritual way. Christianity is the faith of the "starting over." The One who created you can recreate you anew in a spiritual way. The Brooklyn Tabernacle is a church well-known for the changes that have taken place in the lives of many people mainly due to its Tuesday evening prayer meeting. One will find in this loving fellowship Christians who were once drug dealers, addicts, gang members, gangsters, prostitutes, homosexuals and the list could go on. The one thing that they have in common is that their unchangeable history no longer dominates their lives, because there was a moment they gained a new future by accepting Christ as their savior.

If you have not done so, do the right thing now and accept Christ as your savior and get ready to experience a better future.

3. The surest way to have an empty life is to fill it full of things. – Unknown

In 1980, millionaire Malcom Forbes said, "He who dies with the most toys wins." This connotes a philosophy of pure materialism. As deplorable as this is, it is safe to say this is what many people base their life on today. Those who live in America, and for that matter in any developed nation, are bombarded daily with advertisements trying to entice people to get more stuff. These things are pedaled to make us more acceptable to others, give us higher self-esteem, and reveal our successful life, in short, deliver true happiness.

The truth is, things don't do this. The formula followed is "Get rich, get stuff, and know happiness." Millions follow this misguided creed to their bitter disappointment. Jesus told a story about one such man which is recorded in Luke 12:16-21:

> [16] And he told them this parable: "The ground of a certain rich man yielded an abundant harvest. [17] He thought to himself, 'What shall I do? I have no place to store my crops.'
>
> [18] "Then he said, 'This is what I'll do. I will tear down my barns and build bigger ones, and there I will store my surplus grain. [19] And I'll say to myself, "You have plenty of grain laid up for many years. Take life easy; eat, drink and be merry."'
>
> [20] "But God said to him, 'You fool! This very night your life will be demanded from you. Then who will get what you have prepared for yourself?'
>
> [21] "This is how it will be with whoever stores up things for themselves but is not rich toward God."

God called the man who filled his life full of things a "fool." The millionaire mentioned above died of a heart attack when he was 70 years-old, short of the normal life expectancy. He would likely have gladly exchanged many of his things for more years of life. An American minister visited missionaries serving in an impoverished nation. At one of the church services he heard the people sing the hymn *Jesus Is All I Need*. He later said that he had heard people in America sing this song a number of times, but this was the first time he'd heard it sung by people where Jesus was all they had.

We don't win anything when we die with a bunch of things in our lives. We win when we die with just one person in our lives and that person is Jesus Christ.

4. There are a thousand hacking at the branches of evil to the one who is striking at the root. – Thoreau

America's famed naturalist has penned a provocative statement with these above words. I am not aware of his original intent for this remark, but I can clearly see its relevance for us today. Thoreau's words makes me think of William Booth, the English Methodist minister who founded the Salvation Army, a ministry dedicated to bringing the Christian message of salvation to the poor. Many efforts are made to relieve the plight of those in poverty and much money is spent to fund these efforts. Booth combined benefits to the poor to relieve their suffering with the message that they needed to repent of their sins and accept Christ as their savior.

The Salvation Army has countless accounts throughout its history in numerous countries of people who were once in destitute situations who then became productive and reliable individuals because they were transformed by the power of Jesus Christ as they prayed and received his forgiveness. Whatever addiction they had which enslaved them to poverty was gone. Whatever bitter attitudes they harbored that damaged their personal view of life were eliminated because of their new life in Christ. Those who found Christ through the Salvation Army's ministry were able to emerge out of poverty. General William Booth was one who was striking at the root.

Today in our society, we have many who may not be in poverty, but they have no peace in life. They spend money on various diversions, pills to relax and may even go to therapy to discuss their problems, hoping to find an answer for the inner turmoil in their lives. They are hacking at the branches when what they need to do is strike a blow to the root of self-centered living and surrender their lives to Jesus Christ. The Prince of Peace does give real peace. 1 Peter 5:6-7 says: ₆Humble yourselves, therefore, under God's mighty hand, that he may lift you up in due time. ₇ Cast all your anxiety on him because he cares for you.

Jesus is ready to take on your anxiety and any problem upsetting your life. In your self-efforts you are hacking at the branches. Jesus can help you destroy the root if you are willing to give it all to him and trust him for the answer.

5. The strongest thing in the world is the second hand on the clock. – SF

We have all seen a second hand sweeping around the face of a clock on its way to measure a minute of time. It should remind us of the fact that no one can stop time. Time just keeps moving. Every day that passes takes everyone closer to their last day on earth. No powerful world leader, no military genius, no champion athlete, absolutely no one has been able to stop time from passing. A person may spend a lot of money on pills, vitamins, beauty treatments even plastic surgery to look younger, but it is just a look. The reality is you are the age you are. Time makes you become older until you have no time left on this planet.

The important question is "What are you doing with your time?" How you spend your time reveals much about your character. Is it always spent on selfish pursuits or is a large portion of it used in serving others, and if you are a Christian are you serving in the name of Jesus? I have reached retirement age. I'm on Social Security and Medicare as is normal for a retiree. Some look at retirement as vacation time. I see it as opportunity time. It is the opportunity to seek God's direction as to what ministry one can commit to, without the worry of making it produce a living wage. It is not the time to live selfishly, but a time to find a place to serve God effectively if you have the health to do so.

Time is a precious gift and it must be used wisely. One person said, "You can't waste time without damaging eternity." Time can be wasted at any age. Time is wasted when you go through life not in the center of God's will. This leads to selfish living that always brings diminishing results. Colossians 4:5 states: "Walk in wisdom toward those who are outside, redeeming the time" (NKJV). The NIV translates the words: "redeeming the time" as "make the most of every opportunity."

Examine your life from a spiritual perspective. Do you believe God is satisfied with how you are using your time? As a living Christian on this earth, you are to be a positive asset for God and the work of his kingdom. You can only be this if you are using your time wisely. Invest your time in ways that pay off in eternal dividends.

6. Avoid stupid debt. – SF

These three words hold very wise advice. Every time I taught a college level class, regardless of the subject, I would always give my mini-lecture on "Good Debt and Bad Debt." I was hopeful that the young minds before me would take this lesson to heart and avoid many griefs in life. Good debt is when you buy something over time where payments are made and the interest paid is the price for the privilege of using the item while it is being paid for during the prescribed time period.

There are four main items where good debt is appropriate to obtain. They are house, car, education and furniture. All of these items once paid off still give you equity. It may take a long time to pay off a house, but when you do you have the house that is now worth more than you paid for it. It becomes more than a purchase by being a wise investment.

A car is a necessity for most people for transportation. It is necessary to get to work and meet family obligations. You may not be able to buy a car without a car loan. You get to use the car while you are making payments. As long as the payments are within your budget, this is wise debt. When the car is paid off, it is not worth what you paid for it, since it has depreciated through use, but it is worth something and may be the trade-in down payment for a newer car.

Education may require a college loan that will mean payments will have to be made once graduation takes place and a job is secured. Likely the job will provide income for the loan to be paid off and the education will launch you into a career that will increase your wealth. This also can be seen as an investment that pays off and the debt occurred was a wise strategy.

Some types of furniture do not wear out; chest of drawers, tables and cabinets are examples. If your income and budget so allows, quality furniture can be purchased over time. When the furniture is paid off, you still have it providing the same service it did the first day it came to your house. When there is equity after a debt is paid off it is good debt.

It is unwise to go into debt on consumable items which are totally used up and payment is still being made on them. The credit card has made this type of debt possible. Millions are using it and creating difficulties for their lives. The concept is "buy now, enjoy now and pay later." The problem is the pay later is difficult because there is the desire to add to the debt by using the credit card to have another go at enticing experiences of consumable items. Credit card interest is some of the highest interest there is to pay. Many credit cards are well over 20 percent. When you purchase a consumable item such as a meal, a hotel stay, an airfare and an admission to an attraction on your credit card and do not pay it off at the time when the monthly credit card bill comes, you are going into debt for items which have no equity. There is no existing value from the items because they have been totally consumed. This is bad debt. One financial planner told me he had a couple who had $50,000 worth of credit card debt, much of which was spent on consumable item. There are many people who maintain $10,000 of debt on their credit cards at all times.

Debt is stressful. It has been the reason for many divorces and the cause of unhappiness in many marriages even if divorce was avoided. Living within your means is wise advice even if it means you delay owning the most updated iphone or put off a grand vacation to a later time. We learned earlier how you manage your time reveals a lot about your character. The same can be said for your money. The Bible clearly spells out a Christian should tithe, giving 10 percent to God (Malachi 3:7-12). It also gives a warning to debt. Proverbs 22:7 says: ... the borrower is slave to the lender. Debt is not wrong when it is used wisely. However, the Christian is to be a disciple of Christ and is to order his or her life in a way that serves the Lord. Purchases of consumable items to fulfill selfish desires are neither wise nor pleasing to God.

7. It's nice to be important, but it's more important to be nice. – Jim Feazel

My father taught me this truth when I was a teenager and I have never forgotten it. For a Christian, people count; they are valuable. They have been created by God and He loves each one very much. The sacrifice Jesus made on the cross for salvation He made for all people. It is the responsibility of each person to individually accept Christ's atonement for their sin.

Being nice is a basic virtue for a Christian. Jesus said, "A new command I give you: Love one another. As I have loved you, so you must love one another. By this everyone will know that you are my disciples, if you love one another." (John 3:34-35) Love is the identity badge of the Christian.

Paul stresses the need for love and kindness when he writes about the fruit of the spirit in Galatians 5:

> $_{22}$ But the fruit of the Spirit is love, joy, peace, forbearance, kindness, goodness, faithfulness, $_{23}$ gentleness and self-control. Against such things there is no law. $_{24}$Those who belong to Christ Jesus have crucified the flesh with its passions and desires. $_{25}$ Since we live by the Spirit, let us keep in step with the Spirit. $_{26}$ Let us not become conceited, provoking and envying each other.

My father only had a 10th grade education, but he had wisdom to impart to his sons. I highly treasure the advice in this thought. It is my hope that as I show the fruit of the spirit in my life that others will want to know the source and I can point them to the one who died for them to forgive them of their sins.

8. Put treasures in heaven. – Jesus (Matthew 6:19-21)

We looked at the topic of materialism earlier. Jesus is clearly opposed to it. He said in Matthew 6:9-21:

> $_{19}$ "Do not store up for yourselves treasures on earth, where moths and vermin destroy, and where thieves break in and steal. $_{20}$ But store up for yourselves treasures in heaven, where moths and vermin do not destroy, and where thieves do not break in and steal. $_{21}$ For where your treasure is, there your heart will be also.

Some preach a gospel contrary to these words of Jesus. It is called the prosperity gospel claiming health and wealth are the rights of a Christian. They believe that people should have faith to make financial contributions to their ministries in significant ways and God will be obligated to bless them monetarily and in physical wellness. In essence, this makes God the servant of the person instead of the other way around.

We are to put treasures in heaven and not use the spiritual benefits of a relationship with God to enhance our quest to fulfill our selfish desires. We put treasures in heaven by bringing people to a saving knowledge of Jesus Christ not by seeing how much wealth we can accumulate for ourselves and then think we have reached the peak of humility by giving Him all the credit for our good fortune. No disciple lived to be a rich man as we measure wealth today. All but John died a martyr's death. That is not health and wealth. The words, "For where your treasure is, there your heart will be also" are insightful. If you serve God for health and wealth you do so out of greed and that is not a virtue; it is a sin. Those who follow this concept have their hearts in this world and not in God's purpose.

We are to be faithful to the task that God calls us to do so that we can lead others to heaven and enjoy it with them. People go to heaven, not things and they are the treasures we are to place there.

9. Don't throw the big fish back because you think it won't fit your frying pan. – Robert Schuller

I had the privilege to personally hear Robert Schuller give his noted illustration about the fisherman who threw the large fishes he caught back into the lake while he kept the smaller ones. The fisherman's explanation was that his frying pan was only 10 inches wide. Those in the room chuckled at the illogic of the angler. Then Dr. Schuller said something like, "You may have seen this fisherman this morning - in the mirror." He went on to explain that each of us has been given a task or opportunity by God, but as we look at our capabilities we walked away from it. We were guilty of calculating without God.

God is the master at using the ordinary to do extraordinary things. We have to realize when God puts something before us that is his will, he does not expect us to supply all the expertise and skill to accomplish the task. He supplies the needed wisdom and power to get the mission finished. We need to trust him and be steadfast in our commitment to him. Then we can rely on the words of the Apostle Paul in Ephesians 3:20-21:

> [20] Now to him who is able to do immeasurably more than all we ask or imagine, according to his power that is at work within us, [21] to him be glory in the church and in Christ Jesus throughout all generations, for ever and ever! Amen.

Don't throw the big fish back. God will help you find a creative way to fry it. He wants to exceed our imagination of how powerful and awesome he is. Give him a chance and you will find it very exciting.

10. But unless you repent, you too will all perish. – Jesus (Luke 13:3)

Jesus shared this blunt truth with his disciples to make them aware that repentance for their sins was mandatory for their salvation and to escape eternal punishment. Jesus provides no neutral ground when it comes to one's spiritual life. You either qualify for eternal life by repentance and find atonement for your sins in Him, or you must endure eternal punishment. He gives no middle ground.

Just what is repentance? Let's look first at what it is not. It is not some citation of a creed or a voiced prayer which is followed by the same selfish lifestyle previously perused. It is heart-felt regret, deep personal sorrow for sins that you are now ashamed of and are willing to turn from to a new life dedicated to a Christlike spirit. It says in 2 Corinthians 7:10, "Godly sorrow brings repentance that leads to salvation and leaves no regret..." God welcomes your repentance from a sorrowful heart. He knows it is true repentance when you leave your old life and seek the new one he makes possible for you.

We must realize the seriousness of these words that Jesus said to His disciples. Jesus is God. He is the second member of the Holy Trinity, so what He says must be taken as truth. While we live, God is a God of mercy, where repentance and forgiveness are possible. When life is over, He becomes a God of justice. It is either eternal life or eternal punishment and repentance is the first step to life. If you have not done it, now is a good time.

11. He is no fool who gives up that which he cannot keep to gain that which he cannot lose. – Jim Elliot

Jim Elliot was one of five missionaries killed in Ecuador in1956. He was only 28 years old. I became aware of his story as a teenager when I saw the film *Through Gates of Splendor* which documented this sorrowful but inspiring story. He may not have lived very long, but the above quote is one of the most noted sayings in the Christian faith and has touched thousands of lives.

What you can't keep is anything in this life the world has to offer because when you die it all goes away. Money, possessions and even relationships, they all end for you as you pass from this life. What then can be kept? What does not go away when you die is your personal relationship with Jesus Christ. It only becomes more enhanced as you enter a forever life with him in eternity.

Jim Elliot believed it is a good deal to trade a life focused on earthly things for one focused on Jesus Christ as the Lord of life. He used the word "fool" for those who don't make this choice. Earlier, we saw Jesus use this word to describe the man who was so engrossed with his worldly possessions that he built large barns, but did not live long to enjoy his wealth. A fool is someone who knows the truth, but chooses to willfully ignore it to their own harm. Not a wise thing to do.

God's offer of eternal life through His Son is the best offer ever extended to us. We are indeed foolish if we do not accept it. When we have Jesus in our lives as our savior, we have the relationship that we will never lose. Jesus said, "What good is it for someone to gain the whole world, yet forfeit their soul?" (Mark 8:36)

12. Sin will take you farther than you want to go, keep you longer than you want to stay and make you pay more than you want to pay. – Quoted by many

These words, used by many preachers down through the years, have lasted long because they are true. Sin is very deceptive. We think we can handle it. We may know it's wrong, but we think we can break free of it whenever we want to. It doesn't work that way. Sin easily becomes a master and makes us the slave. Paul says in Romans 6:20, "When you were slaves to sin, you were free from the control of righteousness."

The addict never thought he or she would become an addict, but that became their reality. Sin does have a price that can be very high. Some people, because of their sin, have lost their family, their health, and their lives. It was a price that never came to mind when the sin was first committed.

If you have sin mastering your life today, the good news is you can change it. Paul writes in in Romans 6:22, "But now that you have been set free from sin and have become slaves of God, the benefit you reap leads to holiness, and the result is eternal life." Jesus is the problem solver for the worst problem you have in life – SIN. He can end the mastery sin has over your life and lead you into righteous living with eternal life waiting for you when this life is over. You never win with sin!

Unconfessed sin is the only problem that will follow you after you die. All other problems, be they financial, medical or relational, no longer affect you after you die, but the problem of unforgiven sin will.

13. I must first have the sense of God's possession of me before I can have the sense of His presence with me. – Watchman Nee

Watchman Nee was a devoted Chinese Christian. He established churches in China and wrote many books expounding the truths of the Bible. After the Communist revolution, he was persecuted and spent his last 20 years of life in prison. He never denied his faith or loyalty to Jesus Christ. This back story gives his words more spiritual impact. He lived out his faith under trying circumstance.

The two key words are "possession" and "presence." The presence of Christ in our lives by way of the Holy Spirit where we indeed know God is within us is a valuable benefit of being a Christian. God makes it possible for us to go through life in a partnership with him. When Jesus told his disciples they would receive the Holy Spirit some translations refer to the Holy Spirit as the "Helper." Jesus knew living as a Christian in a world opposed to him would be difficult so he gives us a Helper.

We do not get the Holy Spirit by casual connection to the Christian faith or church membership. We qualify for this awesome experience when he truly possesses us. We have to be fully surrendered to Jesus for his Holy Spirit to use us in a powerful way. Kyle Idleman wrote what I believe may be the best book in Christian literature. It is entitled, *Not a Fan*. The premise is that Jesus wants true followers not fans. Fans admire, but followers commit. He conveys that many people go to church as if it were a stadium to cheer Jesus on Sunday morning, then live life without Him in control after the service is over.

The simple truth is that God must have all of you in order to be in you. You must be all in for Jesus or he will not be in you at all. Watchman Nee pens a great truth that God must possess us before we can benefit from his daily presence in our lives. Does the Lord have you, all of you? Are you a follower of just a fan? It is the most incredible trade off we can experience. God gets all of us and we get all of him. Think of the power that means for your life.

14. The key to a long term relationship is "be unselfish." – SF

Selfishness is the main reason for most breakups of marriages, partnerships and relationships. It was the reason man disobeyed the one command God gave him in the Garden of Eden. Satan deceived Adam and Eve into thinking they would become equal to God if they partook of the forbidden fruit. They were not tempted to rebel against God or directly hate Him. They thought they would move up to be like Him.

Since the fall of man, the battle has been "who will be in control," God or self? As we look at the world today and see the discord in almost every aspect of life, it is apparent that "self in control" is winning the day. My wife and I have been married for over 56 years as this book is being written. A young college coed asked me what the secret for making it that long was. My answer was, "Be unselfish." When you demand to have your way, every day you end up losing much along the way. Paul writes in Philippians 2:3-6:

> $_3$Do nothing out of selfish ambition or vain conceit. Rather, in humility value others above yourselves, $_4$not looking to your own interests but each of you to the interests of the others. $_5$In your relationships with one another, have the same mindset as Christ Jesus: $_6$Who, being in very nature God, did not consider equality with God something to be used to his own advantage;

The only relationship which prevents from selfishness developing is the one you are to have with Jesus Christ. Your heart is the Jesus' control center not yours. If self remains in control, you will never know where it will take you but you can be sure it will not be to eternal life.

15. You will always gravitate toward that which you most love. – James Allen (*As a Man Thinketh*)

I once heard a preacher describe a person as a self-made man who worshiped his creator. It comes across as a humorous line, but in reality it is a truthful description of many people. They really love themselves and they actively pursue the things that please themselves. A person who is a workaholic loves the job and the money it produces so much that he devotes himself to it, at the neglect of his family and spiritual life.

Some people do the same with a hobby which they are committed to and will even go in debt and spend most of their free time engaged in it. What you love will get your attention, and a great deal of your time and money. If Jesus Christ has become Lord of your life and the love of your life, you will seek to do His will, in the ministry in which he leads you.

It is okay to have a hobby. It is right to spend time with the family. But, you must guard against anything that would crowd Jesus out of your life. Some people become obsessed with a good thing when they focus on it excessively. I know a person who is so obsessed with having fun that he spends much of his savings on trips and amusements. It has cost him his marriage. When you love Jesus for what he has done, in making you a new person, it is natural that you will gravitate toward him and the work of his kingdom.

In Revelation there are seven churches that are addressed with their positive points and also their failures. In Chapter Two, verse four the church at Ephesus is told, "Yet I hold this against you: You have forsaken the love you had at first." This church was condemned for losing the love it once had for the Lord. If you are a Christian, you must realize that Satan will try to get you to love something better than Jesus.

What do you really love in life? Where do you spend your time, energy and resources? The answer to that question will reveal what or who you really love. Hopefully it is Jesus Christ.

16. No matter what a fan yells or how loud, they can't affect the game, but as a player you can. SF

I am a football fan especially of the college game. Since I was born and raised in Columbus, Ohio, it's only natural I am an Ohio State fan. My dad took me to their games before I was in grade school. I have been alive for seven of their eight national championships. I have learned that as a fan I cannot change any outcome of any of their games. I played football in high school and at a small college. When I was a player, I could have an effect on the results of the game.

How does this relate to the Christian faith? A player in the Christian faith is a disciple of Jesus Christ. When you repent of your sins and accept Christ as your savior you receive the gift of salvation at that moment. Discipleship is far different. It takes time and it is costly. Jesus said, "In the same way, those of you who do not give up everything you have cannot be my disciples. (Luke14:33) Salvation is free but discipleship demands your full surrender to Christ.

Fans cheer; players prepare and become vulnerable when they take the field. They risk injury. In college, I broke an arm and dislocated a knee which later required surgery. Disciples become vulnerable in service for the Lord. Satan takes aim at those whose pose a threat to him. I know from others and my own personal experiences that Satan strikes his blows as one engages in spiritual warfare. He loves to discourage a person in a ministry when the hopeful results do not appear when expected. Sometime there is unjust treatment. Even when you follow the Lord's will and make sacrifices for the benefit of the ministry, you can endure hurtful moments. But you don't quit.

William Wilberforce was very discouraged when he did not see quick success in ending the slave trade in England while a Member of Parliament. He stayed true, enduring all the opposition and repulsive remarks directed his way. It took over 20 years, but he prevailed.

Churches have become comfort clubs with a spiritual tone. The Sunday morning service is the big thing. The desire is to have a good attendance, a pleasing service of good music, an interesting sermon, and a good offering is always appreciated. Then it's go your own way and come back next week. The last words Jesus gave his disciples in the Great Commission found in Matthew 28:18-20 are very profound:

> "[18]Then Jesus came to them and said, "All authority in heaven and on earth has been given to me. [19]Therefore go and make disciples of all nations, baptizing them in the name of the Father and of the Son and of the Holy Spirit, [20]and teaching them to obey everything I have commanded you. And surely I am with you always, to the very end of the age."

The last instruction Jesus gives is for his disciples is to make other disciples who will in turn make other disciples. Jesus is saying, "I need you to be players, not fans." Jesus actually lived the words himself. During his earthy ministry, he spent more time discipling 12 men than he did speaking to crowds. He had more time in his mobile classroom teaching than He did preaching. The percentage of those in the Sunday morning service who are also in a discipling classroom or program I fear is very low and if this is true, it does not follow the Jesus model.

At the time of this writing, my wife and I are both 78 years of age. She has two younger women with whom she meets weekly as their spiritual mentor. I have gotten into writing to provide materials which can be used in the teaching and discipleship ministry of a church more so than from the pulpit. God's kingdom needs people who are players ready to take the field for Him, not fans who want to attend another pep rally.

A fan and a player at a football game can wear the same color jersey, but the player's jersey goes on over pads, because he is ready for game action not game watching. Commit to discipleship and be a player.

17. Nothing is as good as it seems and nothing is as bad as it appears. – A football coach

I was chaplain of a high school football team when I first heard these words from the coach as he addressed the team in the locker room. I have never forgotten them and believe they teach a valuable lesson. We all desire to experience good things instead of bad ones. I think what the coach was saying was, "Regardless of the circumstances, you need to remain sensible."

When success and blessings come our way, so does more responsibility. Jesus said, "From everyone who has been given much, much will be demanded; and from the one who has been entrusted with much, much more will be asked." (Luke 12:48) When good things come our way, we must guard against becoming arrogant or prideful. Blessings produce responsibility. A Christian who gains wealth now is responsible to use his good fortune at the direction of the Lord and not for self.

We all experience low moments in life. Some may even take us to the brink of despair. I think of the story of Elijah who after his great victory over the prophets of Baal was sent on the run in fear at the words of Jezebel. He hid in a cave totally depressed. He was so depressed and anxious he even called for the Lord to take his life. When he made it to the cave in his gloomy state, the Lord uttered some incredible words to him, "What are you doing here, Elijah?" (1Kings 19:9)

Sometimes we may crawl into our cave of depression because we believe everythng has turned against us. I believe Jesus through his Holy Spirit would say to us the same, "What are you doing here?" Jesus promised to be with us always even to the end of the world. (Matthew 28:20) He has given us the power to be overcomers. Paul says in Romans 8:37, "No, in all these things we are more than conquerors through him who loved us." Jesus is the best resource to have when you are faced with problems.

Bad things do happen to good people. That is the reality of living in a fallen world. I once pastored a lady who lost a husband and son in car accidents within two weeks of each other. It was tough, but God sustained her in these sorrowful happenings. She came through victorious because of her faith in God. She didn't choose the cave. She chose life in Christ.

18. You have to play it from the "Heart." – Woody Hayes

Woody Hayes was the longest tenured football coach at Ohio State. He was very successful but also controversial. He made an unforgettable imprint on college football and he had a positive influence on his players. He urged them to complete their degrees and even provided helpful advice after their graduation. He was also known for his generosity to many worthy causes. His career ended in a very tainted way when at the Gator Bowl in December of 1978, he hit a Clemson player who had just intercepted a pass then ran out of bounds near Coach Hayes sealing the victory for Clemson. The incident cost Woody Hayes his job.

His career may have ended in a negative way and he was embarrassed and ashamed for his action. The disgraceful event in Jacksonville that night, as bad as it was, d d not lessen the value of his words recoded at the top of this page. Coach Hayes said these words on his TV coach's show when he was asked the question about an upcoming game with an opponent who was ranked higher and was strongly favored to beat Ohio State. On paper, Ohio State was outmanned. If they were to win the game, they would have to bank on an intangible factor, the belief deep in their hearts that victory could be theirs. No team has ever won a game that it did not believe it could win. Winning starts with believing.

Believing is faith that the positive can happen even when the odds are against us. As Christians, we have the power of the Holy Spirit in our lives. We can play it from the heart, because he makes it possible to beat the odds. 1 John 5:4 states, "This is the victory that has overcome the world, even our faith."

Even in spiritual warfare we can win when we "play it from the heart" because we have Christ in our hearts.

19. Nothing great was ever achieved without enthusiasm. – Ralph Waldo Emerson

Ralph Waldo Emerson was a famous American writer, poet and philosopher in the mid-1800s. The statement above is one of his most popular quotes. You hardly ever see someone who is lazy, disinterested or given to a negative attitude accomplish great things. People who can tie their life's passion to their career choice are usually successful.

Every spring the National Football League (NFL) holds its draft where teams choose college players for the upcoming season. It is an exciting time for these college players who will become professionals. Some will become multimillionaires overnight. There are some players who are not chosen in the draft, but they may be invited to try out for a team. Some of these players do so well, to the surprise of the coaches, that they make the team and go on to have stellar careers. Some have ended up in the NFL Pro Football Hall of Fame in Canton, Ohio. They had success because they were enthusiastic about playing the game and put all their effort into it.

Enthusiasm can be defined as "strong excitement and active interest." This certainly describes these undrafted players who experience success in the NFL. It is interesting to realize where the word enthusiasm originates. It comes from the Greek word enthosiasmos meaning *inspiration* or possessed by a god. We Christians are to be possessed by "the God" through his Holy Spirit living in us. This means Christians should be the most enthusiastic people on the planet, but I have been in churches and around some Christians where this is clearly not the case. "God in us" should result in us being excited about possessing God and serving him. He has given us forgiveness of our sins, the assurance of living forever after this life is over and the power to overcome or endure any problem which comes our way. How can we not be enthusiastic? Victory is exciting! Just watch the reactions of players who win the big game. As Christians we are winners for now and eternity. It's time we show it to the world and do great things for our Lord with our godly inspired enthusiasm.

Galatians 6:9 says, "Let us not become weary in doing good, for at the proper time we will reap a harvest if we do not give up."

20. Persistence can win over talent. – SF

A very successful and famous comedian was once asked for the secret of his success. The one asking the question was expecting to hear about a special ability to write clever lines or some unique stage presentation. The comedian answered in one word – Persistence. He said that when he was moving up the ranks in the entertainment business and hit the disappointments common to all on this journey, he did not give up. He actually believed there were others who were more talented, but they did not last in the long run, because they gave up.

Thomas Edison is a great example of success through persistence. He tried over 6,000 filaments before he found the one that worked to make the light bulb. He also invented the phonograph, the microphone and moving pictures. We have many wonderful things that make our lives easier, because some inventor had persistence. Someone can possess natural talent that is admired and obvious to all, but they fail to succeed in making profitable use of that talent because they had a poor work ethic.

In the previous "Thought" I remarked about how some undrafted football players have been enshrined in the Hall of Fame. There have been first round draft choices that have been total disappointments when much was expected from them. There was a quarterback who won the Heisman Trophy and many other awards in college. He was a first round draft choice and given a multimillion dollar contract. He spent two years with the team that drafted him and had more interceptions than he did touchdown passes. He had a poor work ethic and was released by the team and out of football. The talent was there, but the persistence and attitude were not.

Persistence is something God honors in those who serve him. William Carey is known as the Father of Modern Missions. This Englishman went to India and served there in the late 1700s and early 1800s. He labored for seven years before he got his first convert. That is persistence. James 1:12 states, "Blessed is the one who perseveres under trial because, having stood the test, that person will receive the crown of life that the Lord has promised to those who love him."

The task may not be easy, but the Lord has promised us His presence and His power. We are to persist till the victory is won.

21. The resurrection of Jesus Christ did really happen. – SF

The most important event in world history is the resurrection of Jesus Christ. If it is a reality, it makes everything he said worthy of attention and should be regarded as true. Therefore, His claim to be God is true. It means he is indeed the "way, truth and life" and no one comes to God without going through Him.

I believe it is true and the reason is the behavior of his disciples. When Jesus was arrested, put on trial and crucified, the disciples were scattered in fear. Peter denied knowing Jesus three times. His disciples did not have enough congruity to organize a Sunday school picnic, let alone conceive and execute a plan that would neutralize Roman guards, roll away a tombstone and carry a body to a hiding place. It is a far stretch to believe they wanted to accomplish such a plan in order to start a new religious faith for which their rabbi was just killed. The hatred held for Jesus by the Jewish leaders would then be aimed at them.

The only reason they would put their lives on the line in proclaiming the message of Jesus being the Messiah was that they saw him alive. If Jesus had stayed dead, there would have been no Christian faith spread throughout the world first by His eleven remaining disciples and later Paul. Christianity has changed the world and it has only happened because Jesus Christ arose from the dead.

Jesus said to Martha before raising Lazarus in John 11:25-26: $_{25}$ ... "I am the resurrection and the life. The one who believes in me will live, even though they die; $_{26}$ and whoever lives by believing in me will never die. Do you believe this?"

His question to her is the same that can be directed to you when it comes to his resurrection, "Do you believe this?" If you do believe his resurrection is for real, then you should be living a life that is totally devoted to him just as the disciples did when they were sure he was alive again.

22. Never let emotion drive when reason should be behind the wheel. – SF

You have seen people or may have even experienced a time yourself when you were so emotionally flustered that you couldn't think straight. When you are in such a state, it is not good to make decisions regarding serious matters. When one comes to Christ, it is only natural that some emotion is involved. Joy is an emotion. There is certainly joy when you know your sins are forgiven and you have God's promise of eternal life. The danger enters when one allows their emotional feelings be the indicator of the quality of their spiritual life.

When we come to Jesus, he must get your minds as well as your hearts. I have seen people have an elevator type Christian experience where they go up and down depending on how they feel emotionally regarding their spiritual life. Knowing God's will is important. It guides you to the ministry in which he wants you to serve. Discerning his will takes reasoning by the working of a transformed mind.

Some who have been emotionally touched by a ministry which presents a well scripted television show. They give a sizable donation to it, then later learn that it is tied to a financial or moral scandal. Reason was not a factor in their action. Love is a strong and wonderful emotion. It is important that every married couple experience it, but when they plan their future life together they will need reason taking the lead regarding major decisions.

The apostle Paul said in Romans 12:2, "Do not conform to the pattern of this world, but be transformed by the renewing of your mind. Then you will be able to test and approve what God's will is—his good, pleasing and perfect will."

Knowing and doing God's will, should be the goal of every Christian. This verse clearly reveals that knowing God's will comes from a sound, transformed mind where reason is in the driver's seat. When Elijah took flight in fear at Jezebel's threat and hid in a cave, he was acting on the emotion of fear. God had to remind him that he had prevailed and would prevail because God was on his side. We are not to be Christians because it feels good, but because we know it is the best way to live.

23. Aiming your mind at the right targets prevents many regrets. – SF

Another way to say this is, "Whatever gets your attention gets you." For something to get your attention, you must be willing to allow it to have your attention. Some have aimed their attention toward accumulating possessions only to regret the debt they created. Some have sought selfish pursuits only to later regret the loss of their family. Some have focused on a compromising lifestyle only to regret the loss of health. An old line that says, "A man climbed the ladder of success only to find it was leaning against the wrong wall." As humorous as these words, are they are a tragic description of some people's lives.

As Christians, we must have our aim on Jesus Christ so that we can live a life pleasing unto him. When you live this way you have no regrets. One thing is for sure, no matter what hell will be like; it will be filled with regrets. The problem is that nothing can be done about them there.

Sin causes regrets. The best choice is to not commit willful sin. God gave us a free will. We decide to what we will aim our minds. Adam and Eve caused the fall of the human race, because they changed their aim from God to self, and humans have repeated it ever since. God wants us back and wants us to aim at him. He sent Jesus Christ to die on a cross to make this possible. In Proverbs 3:5-6 we read, $_5$"Trust in the Lord with all your heart and lean not on your own understanding; $_6$ in all your ways submit to him, and he will make your paths straight." This verse gives sound advice as to where we should take aim regarding our lives. If we follow it, we will have no regrets.

24. Plant with purpose, care with consistency and harvest happily. – SF

This thought is relevant in so many aspects of life. When I played high school football I dreaded the two-a-day summer practice sessions, but they were necessary to adequately prepare for the coming season. There was care in planning for each game we played, as we were consistent in our team meetings and on the field practices. These made the harvest of the victories we experienced possible. I felt the call to be a minister as a sophomore in high school. Ten years later, after three years of high school, four years of college and three years of seminary, I was pastoring my first church. Each fall I look at the farm field across the road from my home and watch the harvest. It happens because of the planting and cultivating care which took place much earlier.

    We all want positive outcomes in life, but we must remember they don't come without proper preparation. This is true in the workplace, in family relationships and even in one's spiritual life. It is wrong to expect it to happen if we have not paid the price of purposeful planting and consistent caring. No Christian will harvest a life of spiritual maturity as a true disciple of Jesus without putting in the time to discipline their life to be fully committed. Sadly, such efforts are more rare than common in Christian circles. It seems we have more time saving gadgets, but less time for God.

    We live in a time when so many things come to us very quickly. Meals are microwaved in seconds or a few minutes. There are 24 hour news stations on TV. Smart phones give us immediate information or contact with friends. Our culture does not trend us to long term experiences, but that is what it takes to be an effective follower of Jesus Christ. There is no short cut to spiritual maturity. Let us trust in the promise given to us in Galatians 6:9, "Let us not become weary in doing good, for at the proper time we will reap a harvest if we do not give up."

We must remember that we will not know the extent of our harvest until we share heaven with our Lord.

25. There is no promotion from the will of God. – Mendell Taylor

Dr. Mendell Taylor was my Church History professor in seminary. It was one of my favorite courses. What I remember most from it was this statement he made in one of his prayers before class started. I have quoted this line many times in a sermon because I am so intrigued with its truth. When you think about it there really is no promotion from the will of God. Someone may be the president of a Christian university and another may be a factory worker who teaches the fifth grade Sunday school class at her church. If both know they are doing what the Lord wants them to do, He sees them on equal ground.

One of the last lessons Jesus gave his disciples was about how they would receive the gift of the Holy Spirit. He is to be our guide and our helper. This Holy Spirit, this third member of the Trinity, communicates to us when we pray and read God's Word. He also plants thoughts in our minds that confirms or checks our actions. These subtle spiritual nudges are a way He guides us. If we are not in God's will those nudges become often and prominent. When we are where God wants us and are doing what He wants us to do, then we have peace. If the opposite is true, then His Spirit gently lets us know we are not in His will and we must seek a new course of action to once again achieve it.

Romans 12:2, "Do not conform to the pattern of this world, but be transformed by the renewing of your mind. Then you will be able to test and approve what God's will is—his good, pleasing and perfect will."

Do you have peace that you are doing God's will? If not, seek Him in prayer and Bible study with an open heart and mind. His Spirit will provide the direction you need. Once you clearly know what His will is, commit to it in a partnership with the Lord who makes the hardest tasks more manageable.

26. Life is poorer without laughter. – SF

Humor has always been a part of my life because my dad made sure both of his sons embraced it. I have told people that I wish I had a dollar for every time my dad told a waitress the joke, "Did you hear about the cross eyed school teacher? She had trouble with her pupils." It is a bit corny but not a bad play on words. I always make it a practice to utilize humor when I preached or gave a speech. An experienced speaker once said that it is hard to hate someone who makes you laugh.

I some standup comedy and made a Christian routine which I have performed in 12 denominations and in 12 states and Canada. I even taught comedy at the continuing education department at a Big Ten university.

There was an employer who looked for a sense of humor when he interviewed a job candidate. He said that candidates who displayed a sense of humor proved to be better team members and brought less stress to the workplace. Humor is a great way to cope with irritations and frustrations. I guess that must be why there are so many political jokes.

The popular video series Chosen has given a unique side of the personalities of the various characters. It has Jesus portrayed with a sense of humor. I applaud them for this accomplishment. People in the medical profession value humor as a positive factor in maintaining health and even in the healing process. Research a man named Norman Cousins if you desire proof. Humor is an everyday part of my life. I tell people my life is a sitcom and I can't change the channel.

Laughter is a close cousin to joy and joy is what we have in a relationship with Jesus. As Christians, we have the best reason to laugh. We have beaten sin and have the faith that we will beat death. In Proverbs 17:22 we read, "A cheerful heart is good medicine, ..." Cheerful hearts love laughter.

God made us for laughter. We sometimes do it as an expression of pure joy and happiness. We do it when the bride and groom share their first married kiss or when our favorite team wins the championship. Humor deserves to be a part of your Christian life.

27. Prayer is the necessary spiritual nourishment for Life. – SF

There are many great books on prayer by noted authors. They can indeed be helpful, but reading them in no way replace actually engaging in prayer. It is awesome that God has a way for us to contact him directly in prayer and that he desires for us to do it. Hebrews 4:16 states "Let us then approach God's throne of grace with confidence, so that we may receive mercy and find grace to help us in our time of need."

This is my favorite verse on prayer, because of the analogy it provides. We have the God of the universe, who says, "You are welcome in my throne room anytime you want to come in and tell me what you need." Back in biblical times, going into the king's throne room to get an audience with him could result in death if you were uninvited. We have an open invitation to come in anytime we want.

When we pray we get changed. We are not to use God as a vending machine where we make him our servant to deliver good things for us and remove all problems. It is a time where we feel his presence and gain insight into his will for us. It is the spiritual exercise that refuels our soul and spiritual life. Most people I know don't pass up many meals. We need food for nourishment for our physical bodies and likely have the problem of taking in more than we really need.

If prayer is indeed the nourishment for spiritual life, then I fear we have too many skinny Christians, spiritually speaking. Some may be close to starvation. Prayer is powerful. It can move the hand of God. It can bring conviction to the lives of sinners. It can provide spiritual strength to help us have victory over temptation. If it is all these good things and more, then why aren't we more faithful in doing it? Philippians 4:6-7: $_6$"Do not be anxious about anything, but in every situation, by prayer and petition, with thanksgiving, present your requests to God. $_7$And the peace of God, which transcends all understanding, will guard your hearts and your minds in Christ Jesus."

28. God's Word is a vital defense against sin. – SF

Psalms 119:11 says, "I have hidden your word in my heart that I might not sin against you." This Scripture is actually all the comment necessary to substantiate this thought. It has been noted earlier that what gets your attention gets you. If God's Word gets your attention, then God gets you. When God has you, temptation fails to prevail. Temptation scores its blows when we stray from the influence of God. A regular study of His Word keeps us focused on him.

Paul, in his description of the armor of God, refers the Word of God as a sword. In biblical times, a soldier used his sword as a defense to block enemy strikes as well as being an offensive weapon. It would be insane for a soldier to enter battle without his sword, but how many Christians dare to take on the duties of the day without putting the Word of God in their lives? God's Word is powerful. When we have it fresh in our hearts and minds daily, we stand strong against sin. I believe Satan likes to keep us busy, even if it is with good things and even church things, as long as it prevents us from spending time in God's Word. If he can have us neglect our time in the Bible, he will succeed in creating an opportunity for us to stray from the faith.

We are so fortunate to have the Bible available to us in various translations. Bibles can be purchased at a reasonable price. Back in the Middle Ages this was not so. In 1539 the English language Great Bible was to be in every church by order of the King. It was even chained to the pulpit to prevent theft. Sometimes people would gather in the church after regular service time just to hear the Word of God read publicly. This was very practical since illiteracy was high.

If we neglect our time of Bible reading, we do so at our own spiritual peril. Paul instructed Timothy, 16 "All Scripture is God-breathed and is useful for teaching, rebuking, correcting and training in righteousness, 17 so that the servant of God[may be thoroughly equipped for every good work." (2 Timothy 3:16-17) If the Scriptures will help us become "thoroughly equipped for every good work," it certainly will prepare us to not fall into sin.

29. Discipleship is a lifelong calling that demands every resource we will ever muster. – George Barna

Discipleship is costly. Jesus said, "In the same way, those of you who do not give up everything you have cannot be my disciples." (Luke 14:33)

In most churches today, Christianity has been made too comfortable. Salvation is indeed a free gift, but discipleship is costly. Jesus says the cost is everything you have. I don't believe Jesus is calling for an immediate disposal of all of one earthly goods and bank accounts, but he is asking for a total surrender that will require a true disciple to be willing to part with anything if it needs to be done to be in the Lord's will.

Jesus' requirement for discipleship is a far cry from the prosperity gospel. He gives no guarantee for health and wealth. Paul replaced Judas as the twelfth disciple and all but John died a martyr's death. John died in exile as punishment for being a disciple of Jesus. They all gave up all their resources to serve Jesus and made them available when the Lord asked.

This topic of discipleship is one that has captivated me. The Lord told his disciples in some of His last words to them to go and make disciples. The goal Jesus has for those who come to him for salvation is for them to go on to maturity as disciples. They are to reach a level of total surrender to him. God wants you to be all in for Him before he will be all in you. It is only when he is all in you that you will have the power to make a difference in the world and make disciples like He desires.

Too many Christians seem to make Christianity an "add on" to life as they still do everything else they want to do as long as it is not deplorable. That is not how Jesus wants it. Such a life leads to spiritual lukewarmness which never pleases God.

Be determined to be a true lifelong disciple of Jesus Christ willing to pay the cost for this level of a relationship with Him. Christians that seek and achieve this level of commitment are those who will bear real fruit in the kingdom of God. We are to live for His kingdom, and not for this world.

Steve Feazel

30. Friends of good character are wind under your wings, associating with the immoral leads to destruction. – SF

We have all heard it said of someone who had trouble with the law or experienced some tragic event, "They just fell into the wrong crowd." In most cases, it was a choice rather than a fall. We have been created to be social beings and it's natural to want to interact with other people. The people a person chooses to associate with will have an influence on their lives. Groups have values and if you decide to identify with a group, the group values will become your values.

Parents have a concern when they believe their child is choosing to run with a group of friends who have a poor reputation. Some young people have made regrettable choices in friends. Some people in jail got there, because they picked the wrong group to be with at the wrong time. Some are no longer alive, because the desire to fit in with the crowd ended in a drug overdose. Only 18 percent of Millennials now attend church. Many of them were raised in church, but when they hit college the peer pressure changed their values with disappointing consequences.

Paul had two young men who he mentored that proved to be excellent Christian leaders, Timothy and Titus. There was another young man who was also in his entourage who could have had a tremendous ministry. His name was Demas. Paul reports in 2 Timothy 4:10 that Demas has forsaken him " having loved the things of this present world." Demas chose those with values tied to this world.

One of the most important things for a Christian to do and teach their children to do is choose people of character with whom to interact. Proverb 12:26 gives good advice: "The righteous choose their friends carefully, but the way of the wicked leads them astray." Satan will use a person who wishes to be your friend, but who only desires, in time, to corrupt you. Trust the Holy Spirit to give you the wisdom of discernment.

31. The definition of love is rewritten when you hold your first born in your arms. – SF

I wrote these comments on October 31, (Halloween) 2023 exactly 50 years after I personally experienced these above words. I jokingly tell people our first born son, Lance, was a treat, but then when he became a teenager he turned out to be a trick. For his fiftieth birthday he amazed his mother and I by doing a tandem skydive that included a 45 second freefall from 10,000 feet and thankfully a safe landing.

Our second son, and last child, was not loved any less than the brother who preceded him. I still remember that evening when our first born came into the world and I got to hold that little bundle of humanity. I now was ushered into fatherhood and indeed love was redefined as I looked upon him. I can remember when my father saw this new grandson he asked me, "How much money would you take for that baby boy?"

I said, "There is no amount of money in the world I would exchange for him."

My dad calmly said, "See how rich you are."

If you have held that first born, you know exactly what I am talking about. There are others of you who have that awesome event in your future. But, remember, no matter how much love you will feel for that first born child, God loves you even more and sent his Son Jesus to die on the cross so you can live forever in heaven with him. The words of the Apostle Paul have a special meaning: Romans 5:8, "But God demonstrates his own love for us in this: While we were still sinners, Christ died for us."

God's love far exceeds any feeling of love we could ever experience on this earth. If you know the love of God in a saving way, "See how rich you are."

32. But the greatest of these is love. – Apostle Paul. (1Corinthians 13:13)

1 Corinthians 13 is known as the "Love Chapter" in the Bible as it is totally dedicated to that theme. Paul describes what love is:

$_4$Love is patient, love is kind. It does not envy, it does not boast, it is not proud. $_5$It does not dishonor others, it is not self-seeking, it is not easily angered, it keeps no record of wrongs. $_6$Love does not delight in evil but rejoices with the truth. $_7$It always protects, always trusts, always hopes, always perseveres. $_8$Love never fails.

The reason we are on this planet is because of love. God created the first couple and placed them in a beautiful garden to live in a loving relationship with him. For it to be real love, He gave them free will so their love for Him would be by choice. They rejected this love by disobeying his one command. They chose selfishness, and their sin brought about the fall of the human race. Every person born from then on had a fallen nature and a bent toward sin except for one – Jesus.

God loves us so much that he gave us a second chance. "For God so loved the world that he gave his one and only Son, that whoever believes in him shall not perish but have eternal life." (John 3:6) He sent his Son, Jesus, to take on human flesh and be the atoning sacrifice for our sin. Jesus became our sin on the cross causing God the Father to look away from Him so he could again look upon us and restore his loving relationship, if we will only choose to accept this atonement by Jesus through our repentance. This is the greatest offer we could ever receive and it is all made possible because of God's love.

His love, when apparent in our lives, is our identity to the world that we belong to him. Jesus said, "By this everyone will know that you are my disciples, if you love one another." (John13:35)

The Bible describes the love relationship between God and His church as that of God as the groom and the church (his saints) as the bride. We are told that in heaven there will be the "Marriage Supper of the Lamb." I guess that makes heaven one eternal wedding reception, a forever celebration of God's love for us. If you miss it, it will be because you chose, out of your free will. to reject His wonderful love. The greatest love there is. Don't miss out on it.

33. Rejoicing is an exercise that keeps the soul spiritually fit. – SF

We live in a small village that is home to a noted liberal arts college. The college has a fantastic athletic center that cost 82 million dollars a few years ago. The college blesses the residents of the village with a lifelong membership to use all features of this wonderful facility for one payment that is less than what it would cost to join most gyms for a month. The weight room, swimming pool, tennis court, basketball court, hand ball court, and indoor running track are all available to the village residents. I regularly take advantage of this blessing to stay in good physical condition. My doctors have told me it is definitely working. I am in very good health for a senior citizen.

I think God wants us to do all we can to stay healthy since it allows us to serve him better and longer. It is also important that we maintain good spiritual health and I believe that rejoicing is to the soul what physical exercise is to the body. Paul writes in Philippians 4:4, "Rejoice in the Lord always. I will say it again: Rejoice!" One person once said, "Your attitude determines your altitude." What is meant by these words is your level of success in life, be it your career or spiritual life, is determined by your attitude. If you are positive and rejoice in life, good things happen. If you are negative in your thinking, you likely do not venture forth to achieve much. This is not good when it comes to one's spiritual life. We Christians know we win in the end which should make us joyous people who rejoice in life.

Paul says in 1 Thessalonians 5:16-18, [16] "Rejoice always, [17] pray continually, [18] give thanks in all circumstances; for this is God's will for you in Christ Jesus." Some might say, "How can you give thanks in all circumstances?" You can do this when you have the assurance that you serve a God who cares and loves you very much regardless what happens to you. Suffering may be a part of this life, but this life is not all there is. Jesus has assured us of victory and this gives us reason to rejoice. When Moses sent out the 12 to spy out the Promised Land only Joshua and Celeb came back with a positive report of how good the land was and believed it could be won. The ten other spies bemoaned the perceived strength of the enemies and said the task was impossible. It cost the nation of Israel 40 years of wandering in the wilderness because they believed the report of the ten negative spies.

How many churches and Christian individuals have missed great opportunities because they focused on the obstacles and surrendered to "we can't" instead of trusting in God's help and believed in "we can?" You can visit some churches and immediately realize joy is a foreign concept to them. There are others where you can feel the positive joy of the Lord the minute you walk through the door. If you want to have a healthy soul and a positive spirit, practice the joy of the Lord and make rejoicing a habit. You will be amazed at the effect it will have on others.

34. If you are under slept, overweight, and unexercised, it is your job to change. – Dr. Richard A. Swenson

The Scriptures say we are "fearfully and wonderfully made." (Psalm 139:13) God has given us our physical bodies and we have the responsibility to be good stewards. This is especially true for those of us who have no birth defects or disabilities. If you lived in a house that was "fearfully and wonderfully made" you would be foolish to trash it and let it go into disrepair. Sadly, this is what many people are doing with their bodies and many of them claim a status as a Christian.

Some reading this may think this was a pretty good book until the author went to meddling on this topic. I have taken these words to heart personally. I do workout in vigorous exercise almost daily. I have been in the weight room or in the pool when I really didn't feel like being there. I have also learned that you cannot out train a bad diet. For years I was doing strenuous exercising, but was still overweight. That's when I came across the line, "You cannot out train a bad diet." God convicted me and I started eating healthier and I lost 25 pounds and have kept it off for two and a half years. All my numbers regarding blood tests related to the heart have vastly improved.

I don't believe we glorify God by being overweight. I wrote a book with my friend Nick Gaglione, a certified fitness trainer, entitled, *Lose the Weight and Keep the Faith*. I have been to many preachers' meeting where those at my dinner table outweighed the offensive line of the Pittsburgh Steelers. My family doctor told me that obesity was more of a health risk than smoking. I don't present this topic to shame any who may carry more pounds than they should. I bring it to focus, because we have a mission to perform for our Lord and we do it best when we are at our best physically as well as spiritually. If you need to lose weight or engage in other healthy habits, make it a matter of pray and ask for God help. You might even find help from a group of likeminded Christians.

1 Corinthians 6:19-20 states:

[19]" Do you not know that your bodies are temples of the Holy Spirit, who is in you, whom you have received from God? You are not your own; [20]you were bought at a price. Therefore honor God with your bodies." We don't honor our bodies when we are undisciplined in our health habits.

35. Know success by cultivating a good work ethic. – SF

Integrity and honesty must be an important part of a Christian's life. Ethical behavior is related to moral principles. It is bothersome when I heard someone say, "Well, it might not be ethical, but it is legal." As a Christian, when I deal with other Christians I expect to be treated ethically, but that has not always been my experience. I have been unfairly treated as I have sought to publish books and produce documentaries. It is a shame when those who identify with our Lord are not moral in their business dealings. The best advice is to be wise and use sound business practices such as getting it in writing. It is a joy to work with those who do have high ethical standards. You want to repeat working with them.

I was thrilled when my son was a store manager and his boss told me how impressed he was with my son's work ethic. Every employer looks for this and highly values it. Coaches admire it in their players. As you examine your service to the Lord, would He be approving of your work ethic and your behavior? God values these two virtues which too often are lacking in a lot of believers. His word verifies this.

Ethical
Proverbs 11:3, The integrity of the upright guides them, but the unfaithful are destroyed by their duplicity.

Proverbs 12:22, The LORD detests lying lips, but he delights in people who are trustworthy.

Proverbs 21:3, To do what is right and just is more acceptable to the LORD than sacrifice.

Work Ethic

Proverbs 14:23, All hard work brings a profit, but mere talk leads only to poverty.

Colossians 3:17, And whatever you do, whether in word or deed, do it all in the name of the Lord Jesus, giving thanks to God the Father through him.

Proverbs 21:25, The craving of a sluggard will be the death of him, because his hands refuse to work.

36. But among you there must not be even a hint of sexual immorality… – Apostle Paul (Ephesians 5:3)

If anyone was wondering what the sexual standard is for a Christian, this verse above sums it up rather bluntly. Popular practices and an acceptance of relative morality may bring cultural changes regarding sex to our society, but it does not change God's standard on sex. Any sexual activity that takes place that is not between a man and a woman who are married to each other is sexual immorality. When gentiles were converted to Christianity, the Council of Jerusalem placed only a few restrictions and the admonition to avoid sexual immorality.

I think God's standard is beneficial because sex is the means through which people are created. People are created in the image of God with souls that will live on for eternity. We believe there is sanctity to life. If people are sacred, then it seems only logical that the means that reproduces people would be regarded as sacred. Today, sex is regarded as a recreational sport much like a game of golf or tennis. That is not how God sees it. Many heartaches are suffered by those who believe casual sex is the new norm. An unwanted pregnancy will change a person's life plans. Some who chose abortion later regret it and suffer depression or worse. Some acquired a STD. Some of these are curable, but some like herpes are recurring throughout life. In short, God's standard makes sense.

The concept of "not even a hint" stands against the viewing of pornography which, sadly, is a big problem even among people who attend church regularly. Few churches make any effort to deal with it. Jesus clearly communicates that it is wrong: $_{27}$"You have heard that it was said, 'You shall not commit adultery.'[28]But I tell you that anyone who looks at a woman lustfully has already committed adultery with her in his heart". (Matthew 5-27-28) God made sex to be enjoyed by a married couple. It produces children. He loves children. He made sex as a means for two people to become one flesh in total commitment to each other. It is wrong to taint this beautiful gift from God in acts of sexual immorality.

37. When the righteous thrive, the people rejoice; when the wicked rule, the people groan. – Proverbs 29:2

In the rural county in which I live, we have three major successful businesses that are very generous with their donations to community charities and to the two colleges in the area. They are proof that when the "righteous thrive, the people rejoice. Sadly, the last half of the above verse is true and being experienced around the world and in America. There is a lot of groaning going on because the wicked are ruling. Many nations are under the power of dictators and the people are suffering. When this book was written, political leaders in charge supported abortion, same sex marriage and transgender fluidity. All of these would have been opposed by our Founders, since these are against the standards communicated in the Bible.

The darkest day in American history was not Pearl Harbor or 9-11. It was June 25, 1962 when the Supreme Court ruled that prayer in school was unconstitutional. If that were really true, then the men who drafted the Constitution immediately went forth and violated it. The Founders stood with Noah Webster who said. "In my view, the Christian religion is the most important and one of the first things in which all children, under a free government ought to be instructed." He also stated, "Education is useless without the Bible. The Bible was America's basic text book in all fields. God's Word, contained in the Bible, has furnished all necessary rules to direct our conduct."

A casual study of America history reveals the United States was founded with a Christian Heritage. I wrote a book with Mike Huckabee entitled, *The Three Cs that Made America Great: Christianity, Capitalism and the Constitution*. These three foundation stones of our nation are now under attack and people are groaning.

Psalm 33:12 says, "Blessed is the nation whose God is the Lord, ..." The "separation of church and state" was never the goal of our Founders. God was at the heart of our nation at its founding. The Declaration of Independence states that we have unalienable rights given to us by our Creator. Some say "religion and politics don't mix." Our Founders believed that religion and politics not only mixed, but that religion was a necessary foundation for a political system. The religion for them was Christianity. I believe a Christian should vote for the candidate and political party that comes the closest to upholding Christian principles and values. This would make for less groaning.

38. Whoever believes in the Son has eternal life, but whoever rejects the Son will not see life, for God's wrath remains on him. – Jesus (John 3:36)

We have already looked at the reality of the resurrection of Jesus Christ which merits our attention to all the things he has said. His above words are very serious and call for us to make an equally serious choice. The key word is "believes." One might think that Jesus just means believing he exists and had a history on this earth. The meaning is a little deeper than that. In says in James 2:19, "You believe that there is one God. Good! Even the demons believe that—and shudder."

The demons of hell are not atheists. They know there is a God and they know he has a Son, Jesus, who has defeated them for eternity's sake. The "believe" Jesus is talking about is "saving faith." It is believing that He is the only means for salvation by repenting of your sins and believing that he alone is able to forgive your sins and give you eternal life. If you do not make the surrender of your life to Him in repentance of sin, you are in essence saying you don't believe in Him.

You, by your lack of action, have rejected Him and must face his judgement and the wrath to come. There is no middle ground. You either accept him as your savior and turn from your sin or you reject Him. These words from Jesus tell us there is a heaven to gain and a hell to avoid. It can't get more serious than that. There is no redemption for a fallen angel, but there is for humans. Hebrews 2:3 states, "...how shall we escape if we ignore so great a salvation? This salvation, which was first announced by the Lord, was confirmed to us by those who heard him." These words of Jesus should not be ignored.

39. Faith can be regarded as a constant prayer to which God provides timely answers. – SF

I was watching a college football game on TV when I noticed that a running back had black tape under his eyes that went across his nose. He had something written on that tape, "2 Corinthians 5:7." I looked up that verse and read, "For we live by faith, not by sight." Martin Luther began the Protestant Reformation on the concept "the just shall live by faith."

I began to think about what it means to live by faith. It means that what I believe in or who I believe in will be to my benefit. We use faith every day. I have faith when I get into my car that it will take me safely to my destination. If I get on an airplane, I have faith that a pilot, whom I've never met, will fly me safely to my arrival airport. I even have faith that the chair I'm sitting in as I write these words will hold me up. I also believe on the spiritual side that Jesus Christ forgave me of my sins when I repented and accepted him as my savior. I believe that as I follow him, He will direct my life and provide me with blessing and help when I face problems.

This constant faith in Christ by which I live my life is like a continuous prayer. It is not a substitute for an active prayer time with the Lord, but as I live in tune with Christ I am open to His guidance through His Holy Spirit from which I get direction and answers to problems without me voicing a need or concern. 1 Thessalonians 5:16-18 describes what I mean, $_{16}$"Rejoice always, $_{17}$pray continually, $_{18}$ give thanks in all circumstances; for this is God's will for you in Christ Jesus."

The way we can indeed pray continually is to live in constant faith in our Lord. Life then becomes an ongoing prayer to him. He actually sees our lives as pleasing prayers to him as we live obedient. When we have a need, He provides a timely answer or gives us the peace or strength to deal with problematic circumstances. Jesus said in Matthew 6:8, "...our Father knows what you need before you ask him." This confirms to me that our consistent faith and obedience is a continuing prayer. This is why we should have confidence that we live by faith and are not controlled by fear.

40. The virtues of men are of more consequence to society than their abilities; and for this reason, the heart should be cultivated with more assiduity than the head. – Noah Webster

We have heard the words, "character matters Some may say that times have changed and this is no longer true. Those who believe in a relative morality, which believes in no absolutes and stands against biblical standards, would not see character as all that important in today's secular culture. The man who gave us the dictionary believed otherwise. Noah Webster was known as America's School Master. He believed education was important; however, he believed morality and virtues were more important. Someone has said that prisons have enough graduate degreed inmates to stock a fair sized university.

Webster knew that a head full of knowledge could do much damage if it were not guided by the heart. Character was highly valued by our Founding Fathers. It is what helped to give our nation its Christian heritage and the national morality which made it unique to the entire world. The word "assiduity" means paying close attention to what you are doing. Virtue means a high moral standard. In Judges 21:25 it says, "In those days Israel had no king; everyone did as they saw fit." This verse is saying that virtue was not a high priority. In our society today, the same is true. We have a lot of learned people who marched to their own drum instead of the life beat of Jesus Christ. Our public schools give no precedence to moral standards. We only need to look at our news reports to see that it has not paid good dividends.

Parents and churches need to heed the word of Mr. Webster and make the extra effort to make sure our children enter adult life with virtuous hearts as well as smart minds. It is not an easy task, but one worth pursuing. A nation cannot survive long when a relative morality prevails. Selfishness leads to great sorrow in the end.

41. There is "Victory through Surrender." – E. Stanley Jones

E. Stanley Jones, former Methodist missionary to India and noted evangelist, is one of my favorite authors. His insights into the Christian faith are some of the deepest I have ever encountered. He wrote a book entitled, *Victory through Surrender*, which at first glance seems to be a paradox. We never think surrendering is a means to victory, but that is exactly what happens when we give our lives to Christ. Jesus became our sin offering granting us forgiveness and eternal life. We avoid punishment for our sins because Jesus took that punishment in our place. I call that winning. I call that victory.

Many people look at Christians as if they are the losers in life. They think we need religion as a crutch instead of being self-sufficient. They accuse us of having been brainwashed. The famed folk singer, Barry McGuire, who became a devout Christian once said, "We all are brainwashed, I'm just glad I picked Jesus to wash mine."

If we are to be true disciples of Jesus Christ, we will have to make a total surrender to Jesus Christ and renew it daily in our walk with him. E. Stanley Jones points out in his book that we all have to surrender to something and it will be either Jesus or self. Jesus makes this very clear, "Then Jesus said to his disciples, "Whoever wants to be my disciple must deny themselves and take up their cross and follow me." (Matthew 16:24)

I have known people with skills and talents that could have garnered them much wealth in this world, but instead when they surrendered to Christ, he led them down a different path. The skills and talents were used, but not to the gain of earthly treasures and these followers have no regret, because they have victory.

42. God should be an esteemed guest in your life; don't serve him leftovers. – SF

Francis Chan is an Asian-American who has known success as pastor of a large mega church and a bestselling author. He has also started a group of house churches and ministered in other countries. In his book, *Crazy Love*, he introduces this concept of leftovers in a spiritual sense.

Leftovers are appreciated in our house. They are an opportunity for a quick lunch with assistance from the microwave. However, if my wife and I were having special guests for dinner, we would not be serving them last night's Hamburger Helper. Chan points out this is how we treat our Lord at times. We don't give him the time in the day when we are in our prime. At the end of a hard day, we may skim through a few verses in the Bible then lift up some prayer lines that don't take less than a minute. Then it's off to bed. God is better served when we meet Him at our best.

When the Jewish priests offered the sacrifices at the temple, they required spotless animals. We read words in the Old Testament that condemn offering inferior animals: 'When you offer blind animals for sacrifice, is that not wrong? When you sacrifice lame or diseased animals, is that not wrong? Try offering them to your governor! Would he be pleased with you? Would he accept you?' says the Lord Almighty." (Malachi 1:8)

When we don't bring our best minds for learning while in the Word, we are offering leftovers. I believe all of us can look on a moment in our lives when we have been guilty of this. God gave us His best, his only Son, so we could be redeemed and have a forever life in heaven. How can we not give our best to Him instead of leftovers? It may take discipline and setting new priorities, but any changes made that makes it possible for us give our best to our God is worth it.

43. Make sure your faith avoids the trap of lukewarmness. – SF

Jesus addressed seven churches in Revelation regarding their successes and failures. The church at Laodicea was admonished for its lukewarmness, being described as being neither hot nor cold: Revelation 3:14-16, $_{14}$"...These are the words of the Amen, the faithful and true witness, the ruler of God's creation. $_{15}$ I know your deeds, that you are neither cold nor hot. I wish you were either one or the other! $_{16}$ So, because you are lukewarm—neither hot nor cold—I am about to spit you out of my mouth."

Often we hear, "Something is better than nothing." Jesus did not think this was the case when it came to the Laodiceans. He wanted them either hot or cold. Their lukewarmness presented a serious spiritual problem for them, just as it does on a major scale in churches today. Laodicea was a very wealthy city featuring its black wool commerce. Often wealth has a tendency to make people less devoted in the practice of their faith. The Lord loves those who fervently serve Him as their love is disbursed to others. Those who are cold may come under conviction for their sin and be more willing to repent of it than those who, in their lukewarmness, think they are safe in the kingdom of God when they are not. They seek to serve two masters and that does not work, because with Jesus it is all or nothing.

We are not saved by association, but by full identification with Jesus Christ. People who need spiritual help, but don't think they need help, will not seek that help. That is the danger of lukewarmness and it is rampant in churches today. Francis Chan has provided the most insightful description of lukewarmness in his book, *Crazy Love*. He presents a number of actions, and lack of actions, common to those who are lukewarm in their faith. Here is one that is of a serious nature: "LUKEWARM PEOPLE do whatever is necessary to keep themselves from feeling too guilty. They want to do the bare minimum to be 'good enough' without it requiring too much of them." (Crazy Love p. 76)

Second Chronicles 25:2 is a verse that penetrated my mind deeply when I first heard it. It described Amaziah who had just become king. The verse said: "He did what was right in the eyes of the Lord, but not wholeheartedly." I think this verse is descriptive of a vast number of people who fill churches on Sunday. They want the benefits of Christianity without the discipline of the Christian life. They are lukewarm and I am afraid they do not realize how dangerous it is to their spiritual life. I don't think we'll see revival in America until the issue of lukewarmness is addressed. Lukewarmness has made our churches more a mission field instead on a mission. Review your life and make sure you are not lukewarm in your faith.

44. When you are good to others, you're best to yourself. – Benjamin Franklin

Benjamin Franklin was a unique individual. He spanned many categories in life, printer, inventor, college founder, scientist, author, postmaster and successful statesman. He had wit to accompany his wisdom and his words above are indeed wise. When you first read them you might think they were out of an epistle written by Paul instead from this old patriot of early America.

Franklin actually lived these words and mankind was the better for it. He invented the Franklin stove that was more efficient in heating a room than a fireplace. One of his most notable achievements was the lightning rod that prevented many fires from taking place in houses, barns and churches. He refused to take out a patent on this item feeling it was too important for the protection of people and property that to do so would be an exploitation of his fellowman. He did a good thing by helping to start one of the first fire departments in America. He never went to college, but he founded one, the University of Pennsylvania.

His sacrificial service to his country during the American Revolution, and his wise advice on both the Declaration of Independence and the Constitution have proven to be good for many generations. He was not known for being the most pious of the Founders, but he was very intrigued by the sermons of George Whitefield. I hope they touched his heart as well as his head. Benjamin Franklin was a true example of a "servant leader." That is exactly what the Bible tells us. The Apostle Paul was on this theme often in his letters to the churches as the following verses indicate:

Galatians 5:13, You, my brothers and sisters, were called to be free. But do not use your freedom to indulge the flesh; rather, serve one another humbly in love.

Galatians 6:2, Carry each other's burdens, and in this way you will fulfill the law of Christ.

Ephesians 4:2, Be completely humble and gentle; be patient, bearing with one another in love.

Philippians 2:3-4, 3 Do nothing out of selfish ambition or vain conceit. Rather, in humility value others above yourselves, 4 not looking to your own interests but each of you to the interests of the others.

45. I've read the last page of the Bible. It's all going to turn out alright. – Billy Graham

I wrote the comments to these words in the autumn of 2023 when Israel was at war with Hamas. Dismal headlines and news stories were constantly put before us. The threat of a possible expanding war in the Middle East is unnerving enough, but then add the domestic problems of high inflation, high crime and low morality and life seems overwhelming.

Amidst all this turmoil we can take heart in the words of the famed evangelist from North Carolina. The last page of the Bible gives us assurance of victory from the God who loves. We find these words Revelation 22:12-15:

> $_{12}$"Look, I am coming soon! My reward is with me, and I will give to each person according to what they have done. $_{13}$I am the Alpha and the Omega, the First and the Last, the Beginning and the End.
>
> $_{14}$ "Blessed are those who wash their robes, that they may have the right to the tree of life and may go through the gates into the city. $_{15}$ Outside are the dogs, those who practice magic arts, the sexually immoral, the murderers, the idolaters and everyone who loves and practices falsehood.

Our Lord has promised to come for us. Much of what is happening is what needs to happen to bring about the time for His second coming. The reality is that these words by Billy Graham are directed to Christians. If you have not made Jesus Christ your savior, then things will not turn out good for you in the end. Christians have dual citizenship. We are citizens of whatever country we live in and we are citizens of the kingdom of God, and that kingdom is coming. It might be sooner than we realize.

46. Our religion is one which challenges the ordinary human standards by holding that the ideal of life is the spirit of a little child. – Dr. Elton Trueblood

It was my privilege to meet Dr. Elton Trueblood in person when he spoke at my seminary when I was a student. The meeting was actually a necessity because I was in line to read the Scriptures in chapel. Most readers get the passage the day before and have a chance to practice reading it. I only met Dr. Trueblood a few minute before he spoke so I did not have a great deal of time to review the passage. Since I don't consider myself a skilled public reader, I was a bit nervous. His passage was from a Pauline epistle so there were no hard biblical names or words to pronounce and all went well. I consider it an honor to have had this role in connection with one of the great writers and Christian scholars of the 20th century.

His above quote takes us to basic Christianity. His words, "the ideal of life is the spirit of a little child" at first glance goes against our years of learning and societal norms. We have been taught to learn and gain as much knowledge about the faith as possible. All of that is good and should not be avoided, but the spirit, which is related to the heart, is different from the head. God can use our head knowledge whether it comes from formal learning in a classroom or by experience. However, what is in the head loses its importance if our spirit is not right.

Dr. Trueblood is telling us that we need to be like a child in our faith in Jesus. A child believes unconditionally that his or her parents love them and seek to do them no harm. Children are too young to understand a lot of things going on around them, but still put full trust in mom and dad. Dr. Trueblood's words take us to Matthew 18:2-5:

₂He (Jesus) called a little child to him, and placed the child among them. ₃And he said: "Truly I tell you, unless you change and become like little children, you will never enter the kingdom of heaven. ₄Therefore, whoever takes the lowly position of this child is the greatest in the kingdom of heaven. ₅And whoever welcomes one such child in my name welcomes me.

The spirit of a child gives us a vital basic lesson in living by faith and trusting in God when we don't know all the answers.

47. We can stand affliction better than we can prosperity, for in prosperity we forget God. – Dwight L. Moody

We pray to God for help when we experience affliction, but when all is going well and we enjoy prosperity, we tend to be self-reliant. This wise and famous Chicago pastor knew this and we should take his word to heart. As I read the New Testament, I am amazed at how often the theme of "not trusting in material things" appears. We need things to sustain life, but we must never let the quest for things be the dominent force in our lives.

Paul told the Philippians that some "preach Christ out of selfish ambition." We have some like that today. I addressed the concept of the prosperity gospel being problematic to the Christian faith before and I will likely do so again, because I believe there is ample evidence in the New Testament that it is adverse to the character of Christ. Jesus did not come to give us a perfect life of health and wealth. If a preacher motivates someone to give to a ministry, thinking that it will require God to bless them with wealth in return that is endorsing greed, which is not a Christian virtue.

It is not impossible to be rich and a devoted servant to Christ. I have known several who practice the gift of generosity. In the Parable of the Sower, Jesus warned how wealth can be a problem to spiritual growth: "The seed that fell among thorns stands for those who hear, but as they go on their way they are choked by life's worries, riches and pleasures, and they do not mature." (Luke 8:14) If God blesses you with wealth it is an opportunity to bless others with it.

Paul told Timothy about how dangerous wealth and not surrendering to God can be: [17] "Command those who are rich in this present world not to be arrogant nor to put their hope in wealth, which is so uncertain, but to put their hope in God, who richly provides us with everything for our enjoyment. $_{18}$ Command them to do good, to be rich in good deeds, and to be generous and willing to share." (1Timothy 6:17-18)

Don't be a Christian that allows the riches and pleasures of the world to choke out your spiritual life. If you face an affliction, remember he cares for you and will give you the strength to face it victoriously.

48. Take care of your life and the Lord will take care of your death. – George Whitefield

George Whitefield, a British preacher, was one of the most distinct voices during the Frist Great Awakening in America before the Revolutionary War. He made a lasting impression on Benjamin Franklin as the Founding Father heard him when he preached to a crowd of over 25,000 in Philadelphia. Whitefield's words above are both simple and profound. We must first learn what he meant by "taking care of your life."

Whitefield's sermons were based on the Word of God. He lived his life on that same foundation. He believed that the only way you could take care of your life was to give it back to the One who created it. To live selfishly following personal gain and worldly pleasures is not taking care of your life. That is the formula for destroying your life. Someone has said that the death rate in this world is 100 percent. Ever since Jesus ascended into heaven this has been true. As long as we are alive, we live in the day of mercy. We can repent and be forgiven. After we die that is not the case. Mercy days are over and judgment looms.

If we make Jesus our savior, he gives us his Holy Spirit to guide us and help us take care of our lives. David writes in Psalm 23:4, "Even though I walk through the darkest valley, I will fear no evil, for you are with me; your rod and your staff, they comfort me." Many versions call that darkest valley the valley of death. As a Christian, that walk can be done without fear, because that walk for those who love Jesus is a step into life and he confirms this, [25]" I am the resurrection and the life. The one who believes in me will live, even though they die; [26]

and whoever lives by believing in me will never die. Do you believe this?" (John 11:25-26)

We have the assurance from Jesus that if we live for Him, when death comes it will be taken care of by him. We have a great hope that is a splendid reality to come.

49. What is your life? You are a mist that appears for a little while and then vanishes. – Apostle James (James 4:14)

This verse has always captured my attention. It did so when I was a young man when so much of life lay ahead of me. With all the years I should expect to live, seeing life as a mist or a vapor wasn't a common concept for me or my peers. Now that I am past the life expectancy in years, this verse is all too real.

For all of us, each day we live takes us closer to our last day. But this does not have to be a morbid thought to depress us. It just helps us put things in perspective that we are on this planet for a short time and we should make the most of it. For some, that means getting the most toys you can as we learned was the philosophy Malcom Forbes. For the Christian it means keeping an up-to-date relationship with Jesus Christ and doing His will as we serve Him and build his kingdom.

At a funeral, I once heard the minister mention the deceased would have a tombstone that would have the year he was born and the year he died carved into it. Between the two there would be a dash, that small little horizontal line. That small line, the minister said, was the man's life. The minister gave a challenge to those at the service to make their dash count for something meaningful. The way that is done is by first surrendering your life to Jesus Christ. A hundred yard dash is over with quickly. That's why it's called a dash. James reminds us that life as a mist is like a dash. It ends quickly in the span of all the years the earth has known. We must decide, do we want to count the things we have in life, or do we want to make our lives count?

Psalm 90:12: "Teach us to number our days, that we may gain a heart of wisdom."

50. We grow small trying to be great. – E. Stanley Jones

Once again we visit the words of E. Stanley Jones. These seven words carry a significant meaning. Greatness is an interesting topic. It seems that those who make it a primary goal do not achieve it. But greatness sends many who just follow their heart in pursuit of doing something that benefits other people. I think of Billy Graham as being great for what he accomplished, but he never set out to be great. He just wanted to know God's will and do it.

There are many who have achieved fame, but fame is not an assurance of greatness. Famous all-star athletes, entertainers, politicians and even preachers, can lose their reputation because of some selfish action or lifestyle that tainted their lives.

James and John, the sons of Zebedee and two of the Lord's disciples asked him for a special honor in heaven. They wanted to have reserved seats one his right and one on his left in glory. Jesus had to admonish them for their thinking and let them know they had trying days ahead as they did his will. The other disciples became indignant with their two colleagues for making such a request, maybe because some of them wished they had thought of the idea first.

If there are gated communities in heaven we will be surprised at who the residents are. I think they will include people who we never heard of on earth, prayer warriors, faithful Sunday school teachers, impoverished Christian lay evangelists from mission fields and the list could goes on. We are to do the will of God. This is what we are to seek, and trust the rest to Jesus. Jesus imparted wisdom on this topic in His Sermon on the Mount, "Blessed are the meek, for they will inherit the earth." (Matthew 5:5)

Once we get to heaven, we will not care anything about how great we were on earth. If you want greatness, love your family and they will think you're great and that might be all the greatness you need.

51. When viewing the tree of success, pay more attention to the roots and not the fruit. – SF

I have a print of an apple tree in my office. It signifies the tree of success. A few apples on the tree waiting to be picked and next to its trunk are baskets overflowing with harvested apples. The apples are easily seen. They are the fruit of success, but what is not seen is the tree's root system. Without the roots the tree would not have been productive. Roots are not as becoming to the eyes as leaf foliage, but they are essential to the tree's life and production.

There are two lines of words on the image. At the top where the beautiful apples are, the line reads, "What people see." Below ground level where the roots are, we read the words, "What people don't see." Success is rarely an overnight thing. It comes from consistency and perseverance. We see the athlete excel and win the MVP award and we marvel. We may view his or her accomplishment with awe, but we never saw any of the hard work in practice when fundamental skills were worked on repetitively. We never saw them run stadium steps in warm temperatures to hone a top physical condition. The master on a musical instrument can amaze us at a concert, but we don't see the hours upon hours of practicing that he or she puts in to be the best.

Hard work, self-denial, a positive attitude, time management, faith, prayer, extra study and coming back from disappointments are there in the life of a successful person, but we don't see them. We live in the time of microwaves, fast food, remote controls and emails. We are used to getting what we desire quickly, but true success does not work that way. Most get rich schemes are just that, schemes.

Success as a Christian takes time. Spiritual maturity is not delivered like a Whopper. Discipleship takes time and self-sacrifice. You may know of someone who conveys a Christlike spirit in all phases of their life. They did not get that way through a casual involvement with Christ. They were all in and were constant in their commitment over time to Christ and spent the time in the Bible and prayer to be sure their character represented their master. The most famous verse in the New Testament gives us the real standard for success, John 3:16; "For God so loved the world that he gave his one and only Son, that whoever believes in him shall not perish but have eternal life." If you have enteral life in Christ, you have achieved real success.

52. There is no way to follow Jesus without him interfering with your life. Following Jesus will cost something. Following Jesus always costs something. – Kyle Idleman (*Not a Fan*)

When you are completely following Jesus there will be changes in your life. My goal was to be a high school history teacher and a football coach, but as a sophomore in high school I got the call to preach. The result was a career with more work days per year and more years to work until retirement. The overall income was also less. But, It was in God's will. It cost me something as the world would look at it, but as Christians, we are not to view life through the lens of the world.

I get annoyed when people announce they are going to do something and then lay the "God card" down. They start their announcement with "God told me" and then proceed to add the news. They do this to head off any doubts that might be directed their way when their plans are dubious at best. Usually these plans bring no hardship to their lives. I once asked a young Christian lady who was blessed with quality music talent, who seemed to not be using it to her full potential, if God ever asked her to do something she didn't like at first. She said, "No." I wonder how she could grow spiritually. She may have been a Christian, but she knew very little about being a disciple.

Following Jesus will cost something, but this truth is not understood by the vast majority who attend church today. We are to come to God with hands wide open and lifted up to him for him to take anything he desires from us. He may choose to take very little. He may choose a lot. Christians have endured the rigors of medical school and answered God's call to be a medical missionary in some third world country. Following

Jesus cost them wealth and closeness to family for years at a time, but they were faithful.

Jesus said important words in Luke 14:26-27:

$_{26}$"If anyone comes to me and does not hate father and mother, wife and children, brothers and sisters—yes, even their own life—such a person cannot be my disciple. $_{27}$And whoever does not carry their cross and follow me cannot be my disciple."

The word "hate" is used by Jesus not in a spiteful way, but in a way that sets him as a top priority. We must do this to know his will and it can interfere with some of our personal plans. It will cost us something.

53. A belief, no matter how sincere, if not reflected in reality isn't a belief; it's a delusion. – Kyle Idleman

Another way to say the same thing that Pastor Idleman wrote is, "If you do not put what you believe into action, you are fooling yourself." There are thousands of people who attend church on Sunday who by their presence and participation in the service proclaim a faith in Jesus. But when Monday comes and they settle into their weekly routine, that faith is no longer on display. They may have sung "All for Jesus," but He gets very little of their time and focus.

Idleman uses the word "delusion." It means that despite what a person says they believe, there is inconvertible and obvious proof or evidence to the contrary. We really don't have a belief if we do not live it. America used to be a nation that was strongly influenced by the values of the Christian faith. Even schools would not schedule events on Wednesday so churches would not have competition for their mid-week service. That is no longer the case. The church no longer makes an impact on our modern culture. Maybe the reason why this is so is because we have not truly reflected the faith we celebrate on Sunday the rest of the week to those we encounter.

As Christians, we are to be the image of Christ to the world as if we were a spiritual mirror reflecting his character to the world. This is what a true disciple and sincere follower would do. There is that old line that preachers have used for years, "If you were placed on trial for being a Christian, would there be enough evidence to convict you?" It is a common saying in evangelical circles, but sadly it is more relevant to the church today than 20 years ago.

Jesus said, "In the same way, let your light shine before others, that they may see your good deeds and glorify your Father in heaven." (Matthew 5:16) We are to shine for our Lord in such a way that others will to know him also. Be determined to live during the week with the proof of the faith you celebrated on Sunday.

54. There are two days on my calendar, this day and that day. – Martin Luther

This famous German monk provides one of my favorite quotes. I have used it in a sermon on more than one occasion. It conveys a message that every Christian should take to heart. We hear many people say they are living one day at a time. It usually is from an older person or someone facing a difficult situation in life. The fact is we all live one day at a time since we only are given one day at a time. We may plan for future days, but we can't live them until they actually come to us.

Just what is Luther meaning by "that day?" And could it be we actually could live two days at a time? The "that day" Luther was referring to was the day of his death when he would be taken to the presence of the Lord he so nobly served. He lived the current day on the calendar like all his contemporaries did, but he was living his life under the Lordship of Jesus Christ where he was ready to meet the Lord face to face if he were called home on that day. He lived for this day and that day knowing one day they would be the same day.

As it was for this Reformation leader, so it is for us. One of our "this days" will also be our "that day" and we must ready for it. We must live every day in God's will, be obedient to him in our conduct and be faithful in the mission he has given us. If we do this "that day" will be a great day. Psalm 116:15 says, "Precious in the sight of the Lord is the death of his faithful servants."

Whenever, I preached a funeral for a devoted Christian, I used this verse to bring comfort to the loved ones left behind. It is a glorious thought to think that God experiences a precious moment when one of his faithful servants departs this world in death. The Christian who dies and enters the presence of God for all eternity has won total victory. He or she is restored to the loving relationship man and woman was originally made to enjoy. Those Christians who have passed on are said to have joined the church triumphant. That's just another way of saying glorious victory over death makes Satan the loser. As you live "this day," make sure you are in a spiritual condition to experience a wonderful "that day" should it come.

55. Are we in love with God or just His stuff? – Francis Chan (*Crazy Love*)

Again we encounter the words of Francis Chan. To me, he is like a modern day E. Stanley Jones. Like Jones, Chan has that unique talent to simply define spiritual issues. His short quote above is a probing question that all Christians need to ponder from time to time. We need Jesus to be the real focus of our love as we continue our walk in the faith. Some people who come to Christ allow their spiritual life to become stale.

They still attend church. They may still do token service in the church, but they are missing the passion of living for Jesus in total surrender as a true disciple should. They love the thought of salvation and eternal life, the peace and the fellowship of other believers, but their love for Jesus is not yet adequate to suffer for Him in the work of his kingdom.

Jesus clearly spelled out the degree to which we are to love him in Mark 12:30-31:: $_{30}$"Love the Lord your God with all your heart and with all your soul and with all your mind and with all your strength.' $_{31}$The second is this: 'Love your neighbor as yourself.' There is no commandment greater than these."

The word "all" is very encompassing. All means 100 percent. Jesus wants an "all" love commitment to him. A spouse would not put up with partial love from their mate. The wedding vows say "forsaking all others." If you forsake all others then your loving attention is all towards one person. As it is to be in marriage, so Jesus wants it in your relationship with him. We serve him because we love Him, not because we get good stuff from him. If you are connecting to the Christian faith to get personal benefits, you are following the wrong motive. We are to love the One who first loved us. Our life with him is to serve and glorify him, not to use him to get things to please us. If we serve him faithfully, the blessings will come, but they are not why we serve. It's the love.

56. Worrying is like putting the car in neutral and stepping on the accelerator. – Unknown

I first heard this line from a preacher who acquired it from someone else. The author of these words may be unknown, but what is communicated needs to be known by all and especially by Christians. We have heard it said that baseball is our national past time. As we look at life in America today it almost seems like worry has replaced it. Millions of dollars are spent on medicines for anxiety. Counseling has become a growing industry. Worry leads to stress and stress has a negative effect on one's emotions and physical health.

The above line is humorous but insightful. It provides a good description of worrying. If your car is in neutral and you hit the gas the engine moves to full action, but you get nowhere. A definition of worry is "to allow one's mind to dwell on difficult troubles." This can lead to depression which is not a place where God wants his people. There is a fine line between concern and worry. When one worries, they think of their problems and do nothing. When one is concerned, they look at their problems and become engaged in solving them.

One experienced Christian once said, "Why should I worry, when I can pray?" She had a good a point. We have the greatest Problem Solver on our side. We are wise to take advantage of his wisdom and guidance. The last words in Matthew are of Jesus saying "And surely I will be with you always, to the end of the age." If Jesus promised to be with us why should we be worrying? We should be trusting in him in prayer and seeking his guidance in making plans while we shift from neutral to drive.

Jesus addressed the issue of worry in the Sermon on the Mount (Matthew 6:25-34):

$_{25}$"Therefore I tell you, do not worry about your life, what you will eat or drink; or about your body, what you will wear. Is not life more than food, and the body more than clothes? $_{26}$Look at the birds of the air; they do not sow or reap or store away in barns, and yet your heavenly Father feeds them. Are you not much more valuable than they? $_{27}$Can any one of you by worrying add a single hour to your life?

$_{28}$"And why do you worry about clothes? See how the flowers of the field grow. They do not labor or spin. $_{29}$Yet I tell you that not even Solomon in all his splendor was dressed like one of these. $_{30}$If that is how God clothes the grass of the field, which is here today and tomorrow is thrown into the fire, will he not much more clothe you—you of little faith? $_{31}$So do not worry, saying, 'What shall we eat?' or 'What shall we drink?' or 'What shall we wear?' $_{32}$For the pagans run after all these things, and your heavenly Father knows that you need them. $_{33}$But seek first his kingdom and his righteousness, and all these things will be given to you as well. $_{34}$Therefore do not worry about tomorrow, for tomorrow will worry about itself. Each day has enough trouble of its own.

57. God did not create hurry. – Finnish Proverb

We looked at worry and a word the rhymes with it is hurry. God is not the author of hurry, but Satan loves it. If Satan can get someone in a hurry, odds are in his favor that a person will make an unwise decision or action. God is very patient. He proves this over and over as he puts up with our imperfections. We disappoint him in our lives, but he gives us another chance.

We are urged to embrace hurry in life. The TV commercial tells us to hurry because the fantastic offer will not last. Sometimes hurry is the result of bad habits. We don't use time wisely and then it's hurry to church or to some event the kids are in. Hurry has one thing in common with worry, it produces stress. This is stress that can be avoided if we plan correctly and trust in God. When Elijah packed it in and ran to seclusion after his victory over Baal's prophets because Jezebel marked him for death, he combined worry and hurry together, resulting in bad decisions. He had stress that led to depression. It took an encounter with God to make him realize that God was enough of a resource to prevail over his problems.

Crises may come in life, but it is rather disheartening when they are caused by poor planning. I have worked with a man who was involved in church events that I scheduled who had no sense when it came to time management. He was always late causing extra stress on the performers he was bringing to the event and to me and others at the event site. This type of hurry does not glorify God. God prefers patience to hurry. The following three verses show that patience is the choice for the Christian over hurry:

James 5:8, You too, be patient and stand firm, because the Lord's coming is near.

Philippians 4:6, Do not be anxious about anything, but in every situation, by prayer and petition, with thanksgiving, present your requests to God.

Colossians 3:12, Therefore, as God's chosen people, holy and dearly loved, clothe yourselves with compassion, kindness, humility, gentleness and patience.

58. Some people think they live in overdrive when they are just overloaded. - Dr. Richard A. Swenson (*Margin*)

Materialism can be a problem when a person tries to gain happiness by filling their life with things, but overloading can also be a problem when trying to fill life with activities. There are families who are run ragged by all the sports and activities in which they have their kids involved. I look at the evangelical church today. It is far different than when I started pastoring in 1970. We had well attended mid-week services, a Sunday evening service and revivals. Today the revivals and Sunday evening services are things of the past. The mid-week service is all but dead. Even church people have put so many activities in their lives that they have lessened their involvement in church services and events.

Today, people are excited about living in the fast lane not realizing that it is not taking them to a quality destination. The children see it all. If the church and Christian faith are not important to mom and dad, then it will not be important to them. As time goes on, some families realize that what they thought was overdrive is life overloaded. The overload causes discord and tension in the family and sometimes its total destruction.

I have seen Christians overloaded as they add more church activities or obligations than is wise to do. This happens often to pastors in small to medium churches who think they must be responsible for all that takes place. Many pastors have experienced burnout when it could have been prevented. Individual Christians and Christian families must periodically review their priorities in life. Sometimes the answer "No" must be used even to church related items. Families that value their Christian faith must carefully plan what and how many activities to be involved in so they don't infringe on their spiritual growth and commitment.

The Apostle Paul wrote in Colossians 3:2, "Set your minds on things that are above, not on things that are on earth." What we set our minds on becomes our priority. We have more time saving gadgets than any other generation the earth has known, but seem to have less time for God. Don't mistake overloading in life for overdrive.

59. There is a way that seems right to a man but in the end it leads to death. – Proverbs 16:25

One thing I have learned in life is that everyone thinks that what they plan to do will work out. The problem is some plans were made using the wrong information. The above Scripture is very perceptive. It boldly presents a serious truth of life. The first couple, in the Garden of Eden, was taken in by Satan on the "way that seems right" and it did not work out well for them.

It is very discouraging today to see churches and even denominations that are allowing things against biblical standards to be acceptable behavior in the church. I'm sure those who are making the decisions think all seems right, but they don't realize that their changes don't change the Word of God. In his letters to the churches, Paul warned about false teachers who proclaimed false doctrines. We face the same problem today.

Another fact that is not encouraging is that nonbelievers are growing faster in America than Christian believers. The rise of humanism with its relative morality and those who treasure the results of science have generated an increase of atheists. They all feel their way is right, but it leads to death, a spiritual death that is eternal.

This death is earned as Paul writes about it, "For the wages of sin is death, but the gift of God is eternal life in Christ Jesus our Lord." (Romans 6:23) Wages are something one earns and deserves. Paul was not the only New Testament author to see the link between sin and death. James writes, "Then, after desire has conceived, it gives birth to sin; and sin, when it is full-grown, gives birth to death." (James 1:15)

Millions of people are living life on their own terms and rejecting God in the process. The end result will be their eternal spiritual death. It is all the more tragic when some of those people inhabit our church services on Sunday mornings.

Steve Feazel

60. Many ask, "What causes poverty?" when they should ask, "What causes prosperity?" Per Bylund

In Bible times, government did not run programs to help the poor. The Old Testament records laws to allow the poor to help themselves. Leviticus 19:9-10 reads, ₉"When you reap the harvest of your land, do not reap to the very edges of your field or gather the gleanings of your harvest. ₁₀Do not go over your vineyard a second time or pick up the grapes that have fallen. Leave them for the poor and the foreigner. I am the Lord your God." During the harvest, part of it was left for the poor to come and work for their own benefit.

Today, the poor are exploited for political gain. They are seen as a voting bloc to be cultivated by government programs that are more designed to keep the poor in continual poverty. Proof of this is America's War on Poverty in the 1960s. The percentage of in poverty is the same today as it was when it was started. There are those suffering in poverty at no fault of their own, but there are those whose poverty is a result of their own bad decisions or demeaning lifestyle.

Before government became the benefactor to the poor, many churches and Christian organizations helped the poor, but they also asked for accountability. Those in poverty were given opportunity to develop habits that would lead them to a new lifestyle of self-sufficiency. If they refused or violated rules of the ministry helping them, then the help was no longer available. With government programs, the benefits keep coming regardless of what a person does. This is not helpful to the person or the taxpayer.

Per Bylund's above words are a new concept for many. His thinking is that poverty is caused by doing nothing and the prosperity happens when a person does something. That something can be as simple as staying in school and graduating, avoiding crime, getting a job and showing up when you are supposed to work.

I know there are poor people that need our help, some have a disability, and others are the victims of some unfortunate event. Yes, we should help them as if we were giving to the Lord himself as the Bible instructs us. However, we live by Paul's words in 2 Thessalonians 3:11-13:

> $_{11}$We hear that some among you are idle and disruptive. They are not busy; they are busybodies. $_{12}$Such people we command and urge in the Lord Jesus Christ to settle down and earn the food they eat. $_{13}$And as for you, brothers and sisters, never tire of doing what is good.

If a person is physically and mentally capable, God wants them engaged in productive work. This would end much of the poverty in the United States and give people the opportunity to give from the fruits of their labor to help those who truly are the poor.

61. Lose the weight and keep the faith. – SF & Nick Gaglione

It is a fact that you do things better when you are healthy. That is true be it your job, your home chores and even your service to God. I teamed up with my friend Nick Gaglione who is a Christian certified fitness trainer. I have seen so many pastors who were overweight when I went to preachers' district retreats and I mean way overweight. If you stroll into an evangelical church you are likely to see many laymen who are overweight. Obesity is at an epidemic proportion in America today. Many Christians are caught up in it.

I know doctors who believe obesity is more of a health risk than smoking. Research has revealed that obese people have a 28 percent greater chance of contracting coronary heart disease. Evangelical churches have no problems talking about the health dangers related to smoking and alcohol, but obesity and being overweight are ignored. It seems like some churches operate as if the pot luck dinner is as much a sacrament as communion and baptism.

A person must burn 3,500 calories to lose one pound. Given most people's dietary habits and their lack of exercise they don't burn this many calories beyond what they takes in a week. In fact, they often can gain a pound or more a week. Exercising is important even for senior citizens. I have made my way to the gym or pool many days when I did not feel like it. My doctors have told me that my vigorous workout program is the key to the health I have in my late 70s. We sing the hymn "Give of Your Best to the Master." Should this not include our physical condition? We have looked at this topic before, but it is so important it is worthy of a second look.

Paul says in 1 Corinthians 10:31 "So whether you eat or drink or whatever you do, do it all for the glory of God." We do not glorify God by overeating and eating poorly to the detriment of our health. The "battle of bulge" at the belt line is hard, but it can be won. Make it an item of prayer and use discipleship discipline to develop a plan and stick to it. You might get some friends dealing with the same problem to join with you in this venture.

62. Availability trumps ability. – Common saying

One thing employers want from their workers is reliability. Someone who shows up for work when they are scheduled is far more valuable than a more skilled worker who is often a "no show." The same is true when it comes to service in the kingdom of God. You can be highly talented as a teacher, a preacher or a musical performer, but if you do not make that talent available to God, it does the kingdom of God no good.

There was a "no show" in the Parable of the Talents that Jesus shared as recorded in Matthew chapter 25. The servant who was given one talent went and buried it. His master was so irate at this action he had the servant cast out "into darkness, where there will be weeping and gnashing of teeth." This does not sound like a good place to be. It was experienced by this unfaithful servant, because he chose to do nothing with what his Lord gave him. This makes these three above words very important. If you claim to be a Christian, God expects you to use the talent you have for service to his kingdom. To ignore this displeases God and places your soul in danger.

In 1 Corinthians 15:58, Paul writes, "Therefore, my dear brothers and sisters, stand firm. Let nothing move you. Always give yourselves fully to the work of the Lord, because you know that your labor in the Lord is not in vain." This verse gives clear instructions about how we should use our talents for the Lord regardless of how skilled we might be. We are to be firm in our commitment and fully engaged in our Lord's work. We can't honor the character of Christ by withholding our talents from service to the Lord. We must combine our aptitude with the right attitude and serve God with all that is within us.

God will bless what talent we bring him. All of Saul's mighty warriors were "no shows" when Goliath made his challenge. A scrawny shepherd boy named David who had a small skill of using a sling stepped forward. A sling was not regarded as a serious weapon of war, but on that day this small boy with a unique talent and God's presence was all that was needed for victory.

63. Actions amplify your character. – SF

We have all heard "that actions speak louder than words," but they also reveal your character. The person of character I admire most in the Old Testament is Joseph. He had unjust things forced upon him, but he kept his faith true to his God. He went from slave to a manager of an Egyptian nobleman's house only to end up in prison because the man's devious wife falsely accused him of sexual assault. In prison, his character won him the position of assistant to the jailer. This put him in the position to interpret the dreams of the king's butler that led to him explaining the king's dream. Joseph became the number two man in the Egyptian government which allowed him to save his family when wide spread famine hit. He did so in a forgiving way even though evil had been done against him.

In the New Testament, we find examples of good character and bad character. Stephen was stoned to death after being falsely accused of blasphemy against the Jewish faith. While he was being persecuted to death he said, "Lord, do not hold this sin against them." (Acts 7:60)

In contrast to Stephen's Christlike character, is the deceitful character of Ananias and Sapphira who tried to convey the offering they presented to the church was the total sum of the property they sold, when in fact it was only part of it. This lie was exposed by Peter and judgment quickly came on the couple. Their grave sin resulted in them being carried to the grave.

Billy Graham with his massive evangelistic crusades was sensitive to always displaying a character that honored Christ. After every crusade he would have his ministry post the financial accounting for the crusade in the local newspaper. He never amassed super wealth from his ministry. Some famous TV evangelists have not been so honest. Their moral scandals resulted in the crash of their ministries and revealed a lack of Christian character.

Please be aware as a Christian you must be sure your walk matches your talk. Your actions reveal your true relationship with Jesus. The following two verses are supportive of this concept:

Proverbs 10:9, Whoever walks in integrity walks securely, but whoever takes crooked paths will be found out.

Titus 2:7-8, 7In everything set them an example by doing what is good. In your teaching show integrity, seriousness 8and soundness of speech that cannot be condemned, so that those who oppose you may be ashamed because they have nothing bad to say about us.

64. ... do not rejoice that the spirits submit to you, but rejoice that your names are written in heaven. – Jesus (Luke 10:20)

Jesus sent his twelve disciples out for some practical ministry. When they can back to report to Jesus, they were ecstatic that they had the power to drive out demons. If I were one of them, I think I might be riding a spiritual high as well. If they were living today, it would be high fives all around. Being able to cast out a demon is rather a big deal. The twelve disciples must have thought they had arrived. They just did a "Jesus thing" and they were exhilarated.

Jesus interrupted their celebrating with the powerful truth of life. It's not about what you have done on earth, but where you are going after your time on earth is done. Jesus told them they should be rejoicing because their names are written in the "book of life" in heaven. They should be rejoicing that they had heaven as their destination. They had eternal life waiting for them. One day, all that will matter for all of us is where we are after this life is over. If you have repented of your sins and accepted Christ as your savior, your name is written in heaven. It's the most important reservation you can make. Once this life is over you cannot achieve it any more.

Many Christians go through life with grand accomplishments. Some may even gain fame among other believers, but the only way they can be considered successful life is by making it to heaven. Jesus is telling his disciples to keep the eternal perspective in all they do. It is wise advice for us to do the same.

The Apostle Peter wrote, "... and into an inheritance that can never perish, spoil or fade. This inheritance is kept in heaven for you," (Peter 1:4) Jesus has prepared heaven as an inheritance for us. This is incredible! An inheritance is what a father leaves his children. The only one deserving of the inheritance of heaven is Jesus, but he's willing to share it with us, He desires to make us family with him. We get to share in the same inheritance God has for Jesus. This is something to rejoice over. We get restored to the relationship God created us for and it's because Jesus sacrificed himself so we could share in the glory of his heaven for all eternity.

65. Have I not commanded you? Be strong and courageous. Do not be afraid; do not be discouraged, for the Lord your God will be with you wherever you go. – The Lord God word to Joshua (Joshua 1:9)

The Lord gave instructions to Joshua who is took command from Moses. These instructions are relevant to us today. The Lord told Joshua to do two things and not to do two things, then provided him with a promise. He first said to be strong and courageous. Strong was related to strength of character and staying true to his faith. It was a spiritual strong, not a physical strong.

He was to have courage because he would face difficulties in claiming the Promised Land, but he would also face criticism from the people he was leading. He already stood against the views of the ten spies who gave a negative report about how impossible it would be to take the land. Only he and Caleb believed, with God on their side, it was possible.

The Lord told him not to be afraid. Fear is a favorite tool of Satan to dent one's faith. I once heard one person say, "Everything you ever wanted is on the other side of fear." The Lord also told Joshua not to be discouraged. If you embrace courage you will likely not be discouraged. Some have started gallantly on the quest only to abandon it, because some problem or circumstance brought discouragement.

The Lord gave a promise that made it possible for Joshua to practice the two positive things and avoid the two negative ones, "the Lord your God will be with you wherever you go." In Deuteronomy 31:7-8 Moses gave similar instructions to Joshua:

₇Then Moses summoned Joshua and said to him in the presence of all Israel, "Be strong and courageous, for you must go with this people into the land that the Lord swore to their ancestors to give them, and you must divide it among them as their inheritance. ₈The Lord himself goes before you and will be with you; he will never leave you nor forsake you. Do not be afraid; do not be discouraged."

The assurance of God's presence is a resource that allows us to overcome the problems we face.

66. The knowledge of God is very far from the love of Him. – Blaise Pascal

Blaise Pascal was a French mathematician and philosopher active in the mid-1600s. His short life of 39 years made a deep impression. His contributions in science, inventions and philosophy left their mark on society. He was like the Benjamin Franklin of his day. He had some very insightful concepts related to the Christian faith. His above words remind us of an important fact: Christianity is more than head knowledge;, it also involves the heart.

A person can know much about God. They could even have a seminary degree, but still not love God. Knowledge does not guarantee action, love does. Those in your family whom you love motivate you to provide for them and protect them. With love there is commitment. Knowledge can be experienced with no commitment at all. This is relevant to the church today, because we have many people in the pews on Sunday who know things about God and the Bible, but they don't have motivating love to move to a deeper level of true discipleship.

The children of Israel had this problem also. Jeremiah 7:3-4 reads, $_3$"This is what the Lord Almighty, the God of Israel, says: Reform your ways and your actions, and I will let you live in this place. $_4$Do not trust in deceptive words and say, "This is the temple of the Lord, the temple of the Lord, the temple of the Lord!" The meaning of these verses is that the people felt safe from any punishment by God since his temple was in their city. This is evidence that they had knowledge of God. Most went to the temple, but they did not put their hearts in true worship to God. They enjoyed the sins of their choosing. They had knowledge in the head, but no love in the heart. The prophet

Isaiah also described Israel as a people who lacked love from the heart, The Lord says: "These people come near to me with their mouth and honor me with their lips, but their hearts are far from me. Their worship of me is based on merely human rules they have been taught." (Isaiah 29:13)

Learning about God is great, but it can never substitute for loving Him. When we love him our character becomes deeply changed. We seek to be like Him and not centered on serving ourselves.

67. It takes 21 days to change a habit. – Common statement

It is a shame that this commonly known fact is not commonly practiced. It seems like bad habits are easy to get into and hard to break. The opposite is also true, good habits are hard to establish and easily abandoned. Some will say this is just human nature, but it is really our fallen nature. The bad is easy while righteousness is hard.

I never could figure out why New Year's resolutions are so important. People make promises to change something or commit to doing something new because it is a new year. I have always felt if such changes were going to benefit one's life, why wait for the start of a new year? Why not do it now? If you want to lose weight, then why wait? Do it now. If you want to start tithing, why wait? Do it now. If you want to establish a consistent devotional with the Lord, why wait? Do it now.

It is never a bad time to start doing a good thing even if it means ending doing a bad thing. Ending bad habits is challenging and it takes discipline, but if we are disciples of Jesus Christ we should be not strangers to discipline. Both words come from the same root meaning. God's Spirit is a powerful aid in habit changing. I have seen many young Christians give up addictive habits quickly with the help of the Holy Spirit.

When we come to Jesus Christ and he becomes our savior, a transformation takes place. We become a new creation in him. If he makes us new, then our lives must be lived in a new way. Old bad habits must be replaced with behaviors that are pleasing to God. Sometimes a bad habit is pursued because of physical attachment, but often habits are the result of a mental or emotional connection. No matter which, God s capable to help you be victorious in making the needed changes.

Paul writes in 2 Corinthians 5:17, "Therefore, if anyone is in Christ, the new creation has come: The old has gone, the new is here!" In Christ we can know and embrace the new.

Hebrews 12:1 also provides wisdom to follow regarding changing habits, "Therefore, since we are surrounded by such a great cloud of witnesses, let us throw off everything that hinders and the sin that so easily entangles. And let us run with perseverance the race marked out for us." If you want to change a habit, God's got the power to help you do it.

68. Trusting God to provide when you are too lazy to work is to mock him. – SF

When God has blessed someone with a healthy mind and body I cannot understand why they won't earn their own keep. After the COVID epidemic ended there were help wanted signs all over, but few applicants for those jobs. The reason was because the government was paying people not to work. The government was subsidizing laziness. One of my favorite comedians is Stephen Wright. He told a one liner, "Hard work pays off in the long run, but being lazy pays off right now."

It is a funny line, but sadly it's the motto some people live by. I personally know some who live like this and you likely do also. Work gives a person dignity. I don't make fun of anybody who is doing what would be deemed a lowly task, because at least they are working to be self-sustaining. I once worked as a job consultant for the Welfare Department of a Midwest state. I was involved in helping people on welfare get training and become gainfully employed. It was absolutely disheartening to see some receive their training then purposely mess up a job interview, or once hired, not show up and lose the job only to come back to the state for more benefits.

God does not like laziness. The verses below clearly establish this:

Colossian 3:23, Whatever you do, work at it with all your heart, as working for the Lord, not for human masters.

Ecclesiastes 9:10, Whatever your hand finds to do, do it with all your might, for in the realm of the dead, where you are going, there is neither working nor planning nor knowledge nor wisdom.

1 Timothy 5:8, Anyone who does not provide for their relatives, and especially for their own household, has denied the faith and is worse than an unbeliever.

Proverbs 10:4, Lazy hands make for poverty, but diligent hands bring wealth.

This verse in 1 Timothy is impactful. Paul is saying that one who is able to provide for his family and does not do so, it is "worse than an unbeliever." That is coming down hard on laziness. But let's take it to the spiritual realm. Are you lazy when it comes to maintaining you relationship with the Lord? Are there things you could do with your time and talent, but you just don't feel like it? We should not be lazy for the One who gave his all for us.

69. The secret is Christ in me, not me in a different set of circumstances. – Elisabeth Elliott

Sometimes we want to play the "if only game." If I only had more money, if I were only blessed with better looks, If I only were younger, If only ... and so it goes on and on. So many people bemoan the circumstances they are in even if the consequences are not of their own decisions. We've all heard the words, "God has a wonderful plan for your life." We must remember that plan starts with us committing our heart, life and soul to him. If that doesn't take place, the plan will not take place.

Elisabeth Elliot (and yes she does spell her first name with an "s") was the wife of James Elliott, one of the missionaries killed in 1956 in Ecuador. Her above words have not been written from the protection of an ivory tower. No woman ever anticipates her circumstances in life will include widowhood before reaching her 30th birthday. Sadly, that was her reality. What is remarkable about her life is that she went back to the tribe of Auca Indians in Ecuador who killed her husband and for two years ministered to them leading some to Christ. She lived the "Christ in me." She did not begrudge her circumstances, she focused on Christ.

When Jesus called to Peter to join him for an aquatic stroll on the waves of Galilee, Peter did okay as long as he looked at Jesus, but when he directed his attention to the waves, his circumstances, he began to sink. It is true that some people have better circumstances than others. That's just how life is in a fallen world. But if you are a Christian you can glorify God regardless of the circumstances. Circumstances are temporal. Bad times don't last. This is especially true for a Christian because even when it comes to death, we pass into life. Circumstances change, but God's faithfulness and love for us do not.

The Apostle Paul did not always have the best circumstances, but he stayed true to the Lord. He states in Philippians 4:11-13:

> $_{11}$I am not saying this because I am in need, for I have learned to be content whatever the circumstances. $_{12}$I know what it is to be in need, and I know what it is to have plenty. I have learned the secret of being content in any and every situation, whether well fed or hungry, whether living in plenty or in want. $_{13}$I can do all this through him who gives me strength.

Paul chose Christ over circumstances.

70. We need to see failure as a road sign not a stop sign. – SF

People who have never failed at something are people who have never tried to do anything. When I dared to write a book in hopes of being published, I failed for a long time. It took 14 years before the book was published with a coauthor that had a well-known name. Four years later, I did the same with a coauthor with even greater recognition. The experience made me a bestselling author.

At a writers' conference, I heard an author and literary agent tell his publication story. His novel and was turned down 106 times. Later, his 106th turn down contacted him again and said that he had reconsidered and would publish the book. Every studio but one turned down Star Wars. Sometimes it takes years for someone to be an overnight success. Abraham Lincoln lost four elections for either the House, vice president or the Senate before he was elected president.

Successful people use failure as road signs to get directions, not as exit signs to leave the road. When I look at the Christian faith today, I see too many people taking the exit ramp. They think living the Christian life is too hard. They are right if they are trying to live it by themselves. Many of the heroes of the faith have encountered failure. John Wesley went to America to be a missionary in Georgia and by his own admission failed miserably. This experience showed him that he had personal spiritual issues that had to be settled before he could ever have an effective ministry. He had an experience at a service on Aldersgate Street in London where he made his complete surrender to God. He considered this his true conversion. His ministry then became a success.

"Failing forward" means a person learns from their mistakes. Jesus' disciples went from being cowards when their Lord was arrested and crucified to being bold proclaimers of the faith after his resurrection. One of the greatest failures was King David when he committed adultery with Bathsheba. Psalm 51 records his prayer of repentance. He was restored and God called him "a man after his own heart."

We should take Psalm 145:15 to heart, "The Lord upholds all who fall and lifts up all who are bowed down." If you ever fail in your spiritual walk, don't quit. Come back to the Lord. He will forgive and restore.

71. When one accepts the secular worldview that the final reality is only material or energy shaped by chance, then human life is lowered to the level of animal existence. – Francis Schaeffer

Francis Schaeffer wrote these words in 1984, 11 years after the Supreme Court ruled abortion to be legal. Schaeffer believed that if you cannot take a stand for life, you likely won't take a stand for anything. As I write these comments, it is close to 40 years since Schaffer's quote. The situation regarding the issue of protecting life, unborn and otherwise, has not gotten better even though the Court has reversed Roe v Wade and sent it to the states to decide. The side of life has not fared well on state initiatives where it has not won any through 2023. It seems that the public is okay with abortion being legal to some degree.

Humanism, which believes there is no God, is winning the day in America. The segment of population that identifies as "nonbelievers" is growing faster than Christians. If you believe there is no God, then human life is nothing more than animal life on a higher level, but animal life nonetheless. If we are animal life and there is no heaven to win and no hell to avoid, then it is simply lights out when death comes. There is no sanctity of life. Not only is abortion a natural course of action, but so is euthanasia. Some states have legalized consensual termination of the elderly. In Canada the government even encourages it. Why have old people around who are non-producers? They consume resources and pay little in taxes. If we are animals, why not put a person down who is inactive and suffering from the results of old age or even a young person who suffers from a malady that makes a quality life impossible like we do a beloved pet?

Our respect for life in America has eroded way faster than I ever would have believed it could have in my lifetime. One reason is because we, in the church, who call ourselves Christians, have not held the ground. We no longer make an impact on the culture of the nation. We are worse off and the generations after us will suffer because of it. Psalm 139:13-14 records the words of David:

$_{13}$ For you created my inmost being; you knit me together in my mother's womb. $_{14}$I praise you because I am fearfully and wonderfully made;   your works are wonderful, I know that full well.

The Scriptures state that God called the prophets Isaiah (Isaiah 49:1-2) and Jeremiah (Jeremiah 1:5) to their mission in life when they were still in their mothers' wombs. God's support for the unborn is well founded in his Word. To him human life is sacred. All humans are made in his image. It is what sets us apart from all forms of creation. Satan despises this and has set out to destroy this concept in the minds of people and he is doing a superb job. However, no matter how grave the situation seems on this issue, we must be determined to believe in the Word of God and stand for life.

72. Too often, compassion is used to override our better judgement and approve of ungodly lifestyles. – Erwin Lutzer

Erwin Lutzer is pastor emeritus of the famed Moody Church in Chicago. The words come from his book *We Will Not be Silent*. We have a heresy running rampant in Christianity today that is even seeping into evangelical circles. Same sex marriage has been ruled legal by the Supreme Court. Homosexuality has successfully found acceptability in the nation's culture and the psyche of many Americans even if they are confirmed heterosexuals. We now see Christian denominations performing same sex marriages and allowing homosexuals to become members and "compassion" is cited as the reason.

The so-called compassion being extended is overriding good judgment. It does so because it goes against the Word of God. We should have compassion for the homosexual, but not in a way that condones a lifestyle which the Bible deems as sinful. We should have compassion by loving them as Christ loves them and wants them to come to him in repentance by forsaking their sin. It is not compassion when you don't tell someone the truth and put their soul in eternal jeopardy.

The biblical standard for sex is between one man and one woman who are married to each other. Any other sexual activity is sexual immorality. No church or denomination can rewrite the biblical standards for sin no matter what trends take place in the culture or become popular in society.

Paul addressed this problem in Romans 1:26-27:

$_{26}$Because of this, God gave them over to shameful lusts. Even their women exchanged natural sexual relations for unnatural ones. ₂₇In the same way the men also abandoned natural relations with women and were inflamed with lust for one another. Men committed shameful acts with other men, and received in themselves the due penalty for their error.

He then added in verse 32, "Although they know God's righteous decree that those who do such things deserve death, they not only continue to do these very things but also approve of those who practice them." The Word of God states the practices or actions that are not approved by God and they are unchangeable. Compassion is not true compassion when it does eternal harm. Have the courage to stand for truth and love those who are captive to sin with a Christlike spirit that can lead to their forgiveness and redemption in Jesus Christ.

73. To admit you are wrong is not a sign of weakness; it reveals strength of character. – SF

I am sure that many others have said words to this same effect. To admit you are wrong is basic to the salvation experience. The Bible says in Romans 6:23, "For the wages of sin is death, but the gift of God is eternal life in Christ Jesus our Lord." When we come to accept Christ as our savior we do so by repenting of our sins, saying we are guilty of doing wrong.

When we die out to Jesus Christ, there is no self to protect. If we make a mistake, we can own it, admit it, make any necessary corrections and move forward with life. There are people who are so self-centered and arrogant that they never want to admit they make a mistakes. It seems to be a common trait among politicians, but I have actually seen it among church leaders.

No one is perfect. The two people in my life whom I would like to be perfect are my surgeon and the pilot of my plane. The fact is, we all make mistakes. We are all capable of doing wrong. Sometimes it is not intentional, but we display good character to admit the wrong and do what is necessary to make what we can right. This is the Christian way and it is amazing the impact it has on unbelievers. David admitted to the wrong he did with Bathsheba in Psalm 51 where he poured out his heart in a contrite spirit before God. Many couples have avoided painful arguments when one has admitted they were wrong. We can't change the past, but we do not benefit from pretending it never happened. God forgives us and we should do the same for others.

Proverbs 28:13, states, "Whoever conceals their sins does not prosper, but the one who confesses and renounces them finds mercy."

Paul gives good advice in Ephesians 4:32. "Be kind and compassionate to one another, forgiving each other, just as in Christ God forgave you."

Steve Feazel

74. No one can serve two masters. – Jesus (Matthew 6:24)

As I was writing this book, I almost replaced this thought with another since it deals with the theme of materialism which we have mentioned already. Then it dawned on me that since Jesus dealt with this topic more than once, then it is right to present it numerous times, because it is just that basic to Christian maturity.

Trying to serve two masters is a real problem in the lives of American Christians today. America is a land of plenty. I know there are those struggling as they cope with inflation, but there are millions who seek to come to the USA who are trying to escape severe poverty. The late, great Rush Limbaugh used to say that America has the richest poor in the world. And he was right. The benefits given to those who face poverty in America place them far above those who are actively working in some other countries.

If a person has the opportunity to acquire the means to live self-sufficiently, the temptation is to believe that they are responsible for their success. This lessens their dependence and focus on God. They may still have their association with the Christian faith, but it has lost its zeal. They may be active in church programs while still trying to excel in the world's concept of "he with the most toys at the end of life wins." This trying to serve two masters leads to lukewarm living in the Christian life. Jesus knew that if one tried to serve two masters that in time the one of choice would be money.

The prosperity gospel is actually adverse to this teaching of our Lord, since it motivates people to use works for God to acquire wealth by the hand of God. Jesus never endorsed such a plan. John Wesley had a great philosophy, "Earn all you can, save all you can and give all you can." We are often too short on the "give all you can."

My brother used to jokingly say, "Money is not everything, but it's got whatever is in second place beat by a mile." I believe for many in the church today, this is their motto. We need to have one master, Jesus and our money management should reflect it. We should heed Paul's advice to Timothy, "Those who want to get rich fall into temptation and a trap and into many foolish and harmful desires that plunge people nto ruin and destruction." (1 Timothy 6:9)

75. Never be afraid to trust an unknown tomorrow to a known God. – Corrie Ten Boom

Corrie Ten Boom was a Dutch Christian who was part of a family that helped hide Jews from Nazis during World War II in Holland. Though her family was arrested and sent to a concentration camp. She survived the holocaust. Her backstory makes her above words all that more impactful. The conditions faced by those in the atrocious camps are unimaginable to us today. Her survival was a remarkable feat. Corrie Ten Boom gives credit to God for making it possible for her to live through this experience.

In the death camp, every day was an unknown tomorrow because tomorrow could be the last day of her life. We don't know what tomorrow holds for any of us. We have our routines and have some idea how life will go. Yes, tragedy could strike and it does happen to people, but it is not the expectation. If you are healthy, you don't expect that death is happening tomorrow. The issues we have can be different than the life and death struggle faced by Corrie Ten Boom in the concentration camp in Ravensbruck, Germany. You may have a sick child, or need a better job or face a relationship problem.

Any of these can make for an unknown tomorrow, but like Corrie Ten Boom we have a known God who has our best interest in mind for this life and the one to come. There are two Scriptures that are relevant to the truth that Corrie Ten Boom has given us. One is found in Romans 8:31, "What, then, shall we say in response to these things? If God is for us, who can be against us?" The other is found at Ephesians 3:20-21:

[20]"Now to him who is able to do immeasurably more than all we ask or imagine, according to his power that is at work within us, 21 to him be glory in the church and in Christ Jesus throughout all generations, for ever and ever! Amen."

We can face the unknown tomorrow, because we do have a God whom we know is always faithful and seeks to do us good.

76. The trouble with most of us is that we would rather be ruined by praise than saved by criticism. – Dr. Norman Vincent Peale

Praise is always more delightful to hear than criticism. Peale gives us a very practical reminder of how to value each. I once was discussing a proposed novel with a publisher. She asked me if I could take criticism. I told her I had football coaches for six years and had been married for 55 years. Add to that a long stint of pastoring churches and it is rather obvious that I am no stranger to criticism. I might not always like it but I do always review it and if it merited, I learned from it. If it was unjustified, I did my best not to hold ill feelings to the source.

One of my football coaches said that he only criticized players he believed could become better and help the team. If you were not being criticized from time to time, that's when you should have been worried, because he had likely given up on you. God conveys something like this in Proverbs 3:11-12, $_{11}$"My son, do not despise the Lord's discipline, and do not resent his rebuke, $_{12}$because the Lord disciplines those he loves, as a father the son he delights in."

I was fortunate to have had parents, teachers and coaches who gave both praise and criticism as needed and were never condescending. If we only get praise we never learn how to improve and one can always improve be it on the job, in family leadership and in Christian service. Paul even says we help each other when we share where improvement can take place, He writes in Colossians 3:16,"Let the message of Christ dwell among you richly as you teach and admonish one another with all wisdom…" Admonish means scold in a hard way or advise firmly. Paul expected that believers in the churches would admonish each other in a caring way and not be vindictive. The phrase "Speaking the truth in love" comes from Ephesians 4:15. "Tough love's" aim is to makes us better not bitter.

Coaches tell their athletes not get caught up in reading the good press clippings of their last game, but instead prepare for the next contest. I think this was what Peale had in mind.

77. Empty pockets never held anyone back. Only empty heads and empty hearts can do that. – Norman Vincent Peale

We visit the words of Dr. Peale again. Dr. Kenneth Grider is a person who embodied these words. He was a professor I had in seminary. He had an impossible dream of going to college, since he lived in total poverty. His pockets were empty, but the dream was still in his heart and he used his head to think in a positive way to make his dream come true. He actually hopped train freight cars to reach Olivet Nazarene College (now a university), which is also my alma mater, some 50 miles south of Chicago.

He sat in front of the administration building disappointed that he could not register since he had no money. A college professor came by and listened to his plight. The professor was so moved by the young man's desire to get an education at a Christian college that he paid for his four years of college. Grider went on to earn a doctorate in theology, be a professor at a seminary and one of the translators for the New International Version of the Bible.

Benjamin Franklin arrived from Boston in Philadelphia at the age of 17 basically a destitute run-away. As they say, the "rest is history" as he went on to make a major contribution to American history. The real poor are those who don't have God in their spirits, no ideas in their heads and no passion in their hearts.

As Christians, we must never calculate without God. A heart full of the Holy Spirit is more important than pockets full of money. Matthew 19:26 records the words of Jesus," With man this is impossible, but with God all things are possible." The words "with God all things are possible" is the official state motto of my home state of Ohio. They are also words that we as Christians should always keep in mind.

78. You may live in a crowd but you meet God and face eternity alone. – Rees Howells

Rees Howells was a Welsh coal miner turned minister active in the early to mid-1900s. His biography is entitled, *Rees Howells Intercessor*. My professor of evangelism required his seminary students to read it. As I read it, I got a picture of a true Christian saint. Howells was a sterling example of an intercessory prayer warrior. Whomever God put on his heart to intercede for likely would get converted or get healed of whatever affliction affected them. He was a man who knew how to pray. He also served as a Bible school founder, revivalist and a missionary.

His words above take us to a topic that far too few Christians dwell on today, eternity. It seems we plan and anticipate everything in life but for eternity. Careers are planned for, college for the kids is planned and so is retirement. But many people who attend church regularly rarely put eternity on their radar, when it is the most important thing that a person needs to prepare for in the future.

Have you ever been in a crowd, a very large crowd like at a sporting event in a stadium or at a concert hall? You see thousands upon thousands of people. Does it ever hit you that every one of the people you see will spend eternity somewhere? It will either be in heaven or hell. Howells reminds us of the somber reality that we cross the eternal threshold individually. We may attend church with family and friends, but when we step into the realm of forever, we do it solo.

Jesus did not dodge the topic of eternity. He knew how serious it was. He desires for people to know him as their savior and reside in heaven with him for eternity instead of agonizing in punishment in hell. Matthew 25:46 is a short verse at the end of a teaching Jesus gave on those who lived selfishly and those who were caring. Jesus says, "Then they will go away to eternal punishment, but the righteous to eternal life."

The Lord clearly describes the two eternal destinations that each of us must be concerned about when this life is over. Jesus is the only way we gain eternal life. We must repent of our sins, accept him as savior and lovingly obey him. We then will receive eternal life with him.

79. Character in a saint means the disposition of Jesus Christ persistently manifested. – Oswald Chambers

Oswald Chambers, a noted Scottish preacher in the early 1900s, not only wrote these words, he also lived them. He was serving in the army during World War I in Egypt when he suffered an appendicitis. He would not go to the hospital, because he did not want to take the bed that might be needed by a wounded soldier. The delay for his surgery resulted in complications causing his untimely death at 43.

His widow was an expert at shorthand and copied his sermons and speeches which later went into print. That is why we have his words today. His devotional book *My Upmost for His Highest* is one of the most popular devotional books in Christian literature. Every Christian should have this book in their library.

Chambers is saying "a Christlike character is to be lived with full determination to make a difference." His use of the word "persistently" is uniquely intriguing. It means to continue a course of action in the face of difficulties. It goes beyond just mere consistence. You can show up for work every day and be considered consistent. Persistent people are the ones who show up for work and put their all into the job. They find solutions to difficult problems. They insert new ideas that create new opportunities. They don't quit when things get tough. They don't look to find the easiest way.

Chambers knew the Christian life is lived in a real world that is not always friendly to believers making a lasting impact on culture and people. One must have a character like Jesus. If Christians are to change the world today, they will have to demonstrate a Christlike character in a persistent way. The Apostle Paul knew this and writes in Philippians 2:5-8:

> 5 In your relationships with one another, have the same mindset as Christ Jesus: 6 Who, being in very nature[a] God, did not consider equality with God something to be used to his own advantage; 7 rather, he made himself nothing by taking the very nature of a servant, being made in human likeness.
>
> 8 And being found in appearance as a man, he humbled himself by becoming obedient to death—even death on a cross!

80. If the highest aim of a captain were to preserve his ship, he would keep it in port forever. – Thomas Aquinas

Among Christians today there is too much harbor life. The church building is the harbor and the ships are happy to fellowship at their moorings. Thomas Aquinas was a famous Catholic priest, monk, theologian and teacher in the 13th century. He was regarded as the most insightful teacher of his day. His above words are very relevant. Ships are made for travel on the high seas. They are not to remain in the harbor.

As Christians, we are the ships of Christ to carry his message into the world. We do the mission of Christ no benefit by remaining safely in the harbor of the church. The Lord's command to us is to go and make disciples, which assumes evangelism first. Very few Christians are engaged in evangelism, which is contrary to the Christian faith as presented in the New Testament. The disciples were entrusted with the mission of Christ after the Lord returned to heaven. The world in which they lived was hostile to them, but they did not retreat in fear. They boldly took the message of salvation to the people and succeeded to win many to the faith even when opposition was strong.

Back in the day of Thomas Aquinas ships were powered by wind in the sails. Sometimes wind is used as a symbol of the Holy Spirit. Christians need to obtain a sense of evangelical boldness by allowing their sails to be filled with the Holy Spirit. We will continue to see churches fill with people who are ships in the harbor until there is a real movement of the Holy Spirit. But before that movement can take place, the people must desire it to happen and make the sacrifices for it to be a reality.

It seems unlikely to happen, but it only takes a few people totally sold out for God to make a difference and foster a change.

Jesus knew many will respond if believers will take the message of salvation to them. In Matthew 19:37-38 we read, ₃₇ "Then he said to his disciples, "The harvest is plentiful but the workers are few. ₃₈ Ask the Lord of the harvest, therefore, to send out workers into his harvest field."

Make it a matter of prayer for God to show you how you can leave the harbor.

81. The only ones among you who will be really happy are those who will have sought and found how to serve. – Albert Schweitzer

Albert Schweitzer was a German who excelled at anything he set out to do. He earned a doctoral degree in philosophy, an undergrad degree in theology and then added a medical degree so he could serve as a healing missionary in Africa. He knew what it meant to be a servant throughout his 90 years of life.

God has blessed me by connecting me with well-known people like Mike Huckabee to be a coauthor in writing books. It is also a joy to advise individuals for free who have sought my help as they embarked on self-publishing their books. I admire those who volunteer as coaches of children's teams or even at some community organization. They give of their time unselfishly.

Christians should be the prime examples of happy servants because we get to serve in the spirit of Christ and testify to Christ. I have known people coping with some difficult times, then got involved in some ministry where they served people and things changed. Their attitude became more positive as they gained a sense of value in helping others. It wasn't long before the problem they were dealing with was resolved because of someone they met while they served or as they focused on helping others God blessed them with the right thinking to get the answer to their issue.

Serving in love is highly valued in the Christian life. Jesus Christ set the example: Matthew 20:26-28:

$_{26}$ Not so with you. Instead, whoever wants to become great among you must be your servant, $_{27}$ and whoever wants to be first must be your slave— $_{28}$ just as the Son of Man did not come to be served, but to serve, and to give his life as a ransom for many."

Peter encouraged service among the believers: "Each of you should use whatever gift you have received to serve others, as faithful stewards of God's grace in its various forms." (1 Peter 4:10)

If we live for Jesus and not self, then being a happy servant will not be hard to execute.

82. Let us, therefore, forsake the vanity of the crowd and their false teachings, and turn back to the word delivered to us from the beginning. – Polycarp

Polycarp was bishop of Smyrna, martyred in 155 AD. There is evidence that he was a disciple of the Apostle John. He was burned at the stake for not offering incense to the Roman emperor. At his death he said, "How then can I blaspheme my King and Savior? You threaten me with a fire that burns for a season, and after a little while is quenched; but you are ignorant of the fire of everlasting punishment that is prepared for the wicked." He counted it an honor to die a martyr's death, thus sharing the cup of Christ.

Polycarp would not compromise his faith and gave his life for staying true to God's Word and not bending to the false teachings and the popular trends of the crowd. He lived his words and died for the Word. In the Gospel of John 1:1-5 we read:

> $_1$ In the beginning was the Word, and the Word was with God, and the Word was God. $_2$He was with God in the beginning. $_3$Through him all things were made; without him nothing was made that has been made. $_4$In him was life, and that life was the light of all mankind. $_5$The light shines in the darkness, and the darkness has not overcome it.

Of course, John was referring to Jesus as the Word who came to earth as the Word of God in the flesh. Polycarp could have had this in mind, but also could have been thinking about the truth of the Christian message delivered to him by the

Apostle John. What was certain for him was he would never compromise the truth of Christ for a popular falsehood. Today, in many of our churches, we are seeing that very thing happen. Compromise is damaging the Christian faith. What God calls sin must never be accepted in his church, be it a form of sexual immorality or behavior that discredits the character of Christ. Polycarp was willing to die for the Christian truth. It would be such a joy to see a new wave of Christians choosing to live for the truth.

83. Hell is the highest reward that the devil can offer you for being a servant of his. – Billy Sunday

Billy Sunday was a professional baseball player in the late 1800s. He left the sport and became the nation's most popular Christian evangelist in the early 1900s. He once hit fastballs, then was known as a fireball on the platform when he preached. His homespun sermons, dynamically delivered, resonated with people in a powerful way making him well known in the nation. He could be described as the Billy Graham of his day with a bit more zeal in his sermon delivery. He never had a scandal touch his ministry and he was faithful to his family and faith.

His words above are not a strange topic for him. He would not shy away from peaching on the fire of hell and did not hesitate in declaring it the destination of those living in their sins. Yes, Billy Sunday peached about hell. Now on Sunday we hardly hear the topic addressed. Billy Sunday cleverly relates hell as the reward of Satan. It is what the evil one has as payment for those who serve him. That's how Sunday viewed it. There may be pleasure for a season in sin, but it doesn't last. As a pastor, I saw many people cling to sin when the thrill was long gone. They lived in misery, but still would not choose Jesus Christ as their savior. All they had to look forward to was Satan's reward in the next life. That does not have to be true for you.

In Jesus Christ we not only have eternal life in the life to come but we have peace, a sense of love and the presence of God in us by his Holy Spirit. It is a life of joy even on the bad days of life. Jesus said in John 10:10, "The thief comes only to steal and kill and destroy; I have come that they may have life, and have it to the full." In John 15:11 he says, "I have told you this so that my joy may be in you and that your joy may be complete." He promises peace in John 14:27, "Peace I leave with you; my peace I give you. I do not give to you as the world gives. Do not let your hearts be troubled and do not be afraid."

Life, joy and peace, and yes, as a bonus, we will receive eternal life with Jesus in heaven, a far better reward than Satan offers.

84. We need discernment in what we see and what we hear and what we believe. – Charles R. Swindoll

Discernment is good judgment. It is in short supply in the world today. Many businesses depend on poor discernment by the majority of the public so they can sell their products. Many advertisements tell people they need something when they don't. They are just influenced made to think they need it, so they buy a desire not a need.

Discernment is really important in judging the character of people and evaluating a belief system. There is a lot of deception in the world today and with the Internet there are more ways for deceivers to reach their victims. Good judgment is important especially when it is related to your spiritual life.

As a young pastor, my wife and I attended a special district meeting where the speaker was advising on how to increase the financial stewardship giving in a church. One of the things he proclaimed was to convince people to tithe on what they would like to make, not on what they were making. The point was that this would obligate God to increase one's income to meet the tithe. If the person really had faith, it was all supposed to work. My wife and I left the meeting with far less enthusiasm than the other attendees. We both thought we heard a "crack in the bell." To us this plan did not fit the principles or the character of Christ revealed in the New Testament.

Using God for self-gain is not the Jesus way. How does one develop discernment for effective spiritual living? It first starts with a solid foundation of God's Word. You must know God's standards so you can recognize that which is contrary to them. Next, you must have God's presence in your heart by his Holy

Spirit. Jesus told us that his Spirit would be our guide. Lastly, take concerns you have to God in prayer and ask for wisdom. If some important decision must be made where judgment is concerned, there is no hurry. Hurry is the tool of the devil in such matters. We should pay attention to the wisdom James gives about wisdom, "If any of you lacks wisdom, you should ask God, who gives generously to all without finding fault, and it will be given to you." (James 1:5)

85. Most people want to avoid pain, and discipline is usually painful. – John Maxwell

I have never met John Maxwell personally, but his father held revivals at the church I attended as a teenager. His father was then the president of Circleville Bible College, now Ohio Christian University sponsored by the small denomination of Churches of Christ in Christian Union. His father was a very good preacher so John had a good example. John's words are very true. We have all heard the phrase "No pain, no gain."

When I check in at the desk of the gym for my workout session three times a week, the staff person at the desk will sometimes say, "Enjoy your workout."

I say back, "If I do, I'm not doing it right." I expect to be uncomfortable some of the time in my lifting routine if I want to accomplish my goal of staying physically fit. When I played football, my teammates and I had to undergo the discipline of the coach to be in shape and to be prepared to execute the game plan for the next opponent. Sometimes this discipline was painful, but it was accepted because it was needed to earn a victory. Every military veteran who ever went to boot camp would say they experienced some painful discipline. The Apostle Paul likened the Christian faith to the discipline endured by an athlete and like that experienced by a soldier in 2 Timothy 2:1-5:

> $_1$You then, my son, be strong in the grace that is in Christ Jesus. $_2$And the things you have heard me say in the presence of many witnesses entrust to reliable people who will also be qualified to teach others. $_3$Join with me in suffering, like a good soldier of Christ Jesus. $_4$No one serving as a

soldier gets entangled in civilian affairs, but rather tries to please his commanding officer. $_5$Similarly, anyone who competes as an athlete does not receive the victor's crown except by competing according to the rules.

When you join Christ's team of committed disciples, you will face discipline. As mentioned before, discipline and disciple come from the same root word. When you come under the discipline of Christ you will experience some pain in life. It may not be physical pain, but that can be a reality for some in certain parts of the world. There is emotional pain when friends and even family members reject you because they do not agree with your devotion to your faith and love for Jesus. His presence and the assured victory should be enough to motivate us to endure the pain of discipleship.

86. A person who won't read has no advantage over one who can't read. – Mark Twain

Mark Twain is the pen name of Samuel Clemens one of America's most famous writers in the late 1800s. William Faulkner called him the "Father of American Literature." Twain had the advantage of writing when there were no movies, no radio and no TV to compete for the good old fashioned printed paper book.

Some might think this above line is out of place in a book like this which focuses on spiritual inspiration, but I provides a very important point for consideration. Having the ability to read was the means by which one gained an education in Twain's day and it is still true today. Literacy helps one grow in their spiritual life as they are able to read God's Word and other helpful Christian literature that provides inspiration and insight into God's truth.

Mark Twain puts the person who will not read in the same category of those who cannot read. Today, we have many Christians who simply will not read a book related to the Christian faith. This is especially true of men. Some say they are too busy and don't have the time to read, but you make time for the things you want to do. I think every Christian teen and adult should read Kyle Idleman's *Not a Fan*. This book can revolutionize a person's spiritual life. Reading will deepen your faith and may also be the means through which God may guide you to embark on distinct mission projects or think of creative ways to serve others.

My wife was converted by reading Christian novels by Grace Livingston Hill. Her books presented strong Christian moral values and clearly presented the importance of accepting

Christ as savior. Catharine Marshall's novel, *Christy*, touched the lives of thousands for Christ. Many Christians develop an effective prayer life by reading books on prayer. All Christians should make a plan to read two Christian books this year. Reading clubs could be formed in churches to help make this possible. Paul writes in 1 Thessalonians 5:11. "Therefore encourage one another and build each other up, just as in fact you are doing." Reading the books of those who have much to share that will encourage us.

87. Anger is an acid that can do more harm to the vessel in which it is stored than to anything on which it is poured. – Mark Twain

The vessel that a liquid acid is contained in is called a harness. It neutralizes the acid from rendering any damage. If the acid is poured on a material, it causes severe damage. Mark Twain's quote reveals the destructive power of anger. He points out that it is self-destructive. The vessel that contains the acid should have no fear that the acid would harm it, but Twain says that's exactly what happens when one surrenders to anger.

Saul is a prime example of this. His hatred for David basically destroyed him and his rule as king. Saul's anger aimed at David was a fusion of jealousy and rage. He sought to kill the hero giant slayer to preserve his own power after he had fallen from grace as Israel's king.

Jesus gave a warning about anger in his Sermon on the Mount. [21] "You have heard that it was said to the people long ago, 'You shall not murder, and anyone who murders will be subject to judgment.' [22] But I tell you that anyone who is angry with a brother or sister will be subject to judgment." (Matthew 5:21-22)

Jesus put anger in the same zone as murder. It takes a lot of hate and anger to take the life of another person. It brings guilt and judgment on the murderer. There are people who hold so much anger for a family member based on some incident long ago that they refuse to speak to them. The anger is kept alive for years and does nothing but create misery for the one who holds it. Anger is something you keep as a pet that actually becomes a monster that eats inwardly at your emotional well-being. Some of the best healing that has takes place when people end anger with the love of Christ and forgive each other.

Anger is a strong emotion, and if it is nurtured and amplified, it will have a negative effect on one's physical health. We are wise to heed the word of Proverbs 14:29, "Whoever is patient has great understanding, but one who is quick-tempered displays folly."

88. I can do everything through him who gives me strength. Apostle Paul (Philippians 4:13)

This verse is a favorite of mine. When I moved to a new school district for my senior year and went out for football, I did not have the advantage of the conditioning sessions the other players had before the two-a-day practices started. I wrote this verse on athletic tape and stuck it on the outside of my locker. It stayed there the whole season as inspiration for me and a witness to my teammates.

Paul needed strength to accomplish the mission the Lord gave him as the main voice of the Christian faith to the Gentiles. He had physical needs. Just traveling during the times he lived required physical strength since it was mostly by foot. He also endured persecution and hardships that were physically taxing.

Paul gives a clear picture of what he faced as a minister of Christ in 2 Corinthians 11:22-29:

> $_{22}$ Are they Hebrews? So am I. Are they Israelites? So am I. Are they Abraham's descendants? So am I. $_{23}$ Are they servants of Christ? (I am out of my mind to talk like this.) I am more. I have worked much harder, been in prison more frequently, been flogged more severely, and been exposed to death again and again. $_{24}$ Five times I received from the Jews the forty lashes minus one. $_{25}$ Three times I was beaten with rods, once I was pelted with stones, three times I was shipwrecked, I spent a night and a day in the open sea, $_{26}$ I have been constantly on the move. I have been in danger from rivers, in danger from bandits, in danger from my fellow Jews, in danger from Gentiles; in danger in the city, in

danger in the country, in danger at sea; and in danger from false believers. ₂₇ I have labored and toiled and have often gone without sleep; I have known hunger and thirst and have often gone without food; I have been cold and naked. ₂₈ Besides everything else, I face daily the pressure of my concern for all the churches ₂₉ Who is weak, and I do not feel weak? Who is led into sin, and I do not inwardly burn?

Paul mentions the care for the churches which took a lot of spiritual and mental strength. Many heresies tried to invade the churches and there were the Judaizers who caused confusion. The churches themselves had problems which is why Paul wrote letters to them. He was also mentoring young ministers like Timothy and Titus. Demas was one protégé who deserted him. Paul needed strength for fighting the temptations that directly came to his life. Today, as Christians, we need this same divine strength as we live in a culture that is becoming more Christian unfriendly every day. We receive it by making sure the Lord is living in our hearts each day through his Holy Spirit.

89. I would rather die than do something which I know to be a sin, or to be against God's will. – Joan of Arc

This Young French girl, Joan of Arc, is one of the most intriguing people in history. A teenage peasant girl emerged to become a military leader to restore morale to the French army during the One Hundred Years War. She was captured by her enemy, the English, and after a bogus trial was burned at the stake. The trial was later declared improper and she is now regarded as a patron saint of France.

Regardless of the history surrounding her, the above words she has left our world are very provocative and should be edifying to every Christian. Her words "which I know to be a sin" tell us she knew she was responsible for exercising her free will not commit anything that she knew to be a sin. She knew sin was a choice. Sometimes I hear people refer to committing a sin as a mistake. Mistakes are unintentional, sin is a choice. When Adam and Eve committed the first sin, it was a choice. They did not do it accidentally.

Joan of Arc never wanted to be outside God's will. This French maiden was devoted to her God and her faith. If she knew what God's will was, there was no debate. She submitted to it regardless what it cost her. God's will can demand sacrifice on your part. When you know what his will is and refuse to do it, you tread on dangerous spiritual ground. James 4:17 says, "If anyone, then, knows the good they ought to do and doesn't do it, it is sin for them." You are to focus on "what is God's will for you," and not to be concerned with what God's will is for someone else.

This teenage French female military leader who died in 1431 had a better grip on theology than most longtime church attendees do today. She cared about her relationship with the Lord. She wanted to live free of known sin in her life and always wanted to be in the center of God's will. How wonderful it would be today if we had teenagers who were so committed to the Christian faith. The Catholic Church has made Joan of Arc a saint. I don't believe sainthood was ever her goal. Doing the will of God and choosing not to commit any willful sin was her aim in life. It is an example we would do well to follow.

90. Resentment is like drinking poison and waiting for the other person to die. – Saint Augustine

Jerome Augustine was converted to Christianity in 386 and became one of the most influential theologians and philosophers of the church. His words may have touched Mark Twain, since Mr. Twain's take on anger is closely aligned with Augustine's explanation of resentment. I believe that "Resentment" is just another way to spell "Hate" using more letters. Some people have really honed the skill to hold a grudge.

Some people today are living miserable lives because they resent someone else. The person who is the object of their hatred may be totally unaware, and not affected by the malice directed toward them, but the one who holds it is being eaten alive.

We live in a fallen world. Unjust things can happen. Someone can purposely take advantage of you. It can cause hurt to you. There may be no recourse for you to right the injustice. The person may be long gone where they cannot be confronted. You have two actions, continue to hold resentment or let it go. Harbored resentment can be destructive to every aspect of your life. If you want to stop the damage, you must let it go. You are better off taking the focus and energy spent on resentment and putting it into a new endeavor or worthy project that can bring your life positive results.

As Christians, we have the advantage of God's Word and his direction regarding these matters. Romans 12:19 states, "Do not take revenge, my dear friends, but leave room for God's wrath, for it is written: 'It is mine to avenge; I will repay, "says the Lord.'" If someone has done us wrong and never repents of it, the Lord has taken note and judgment is coming in the future. We can let go of resentment and trust our Lord with the issue.

There is another Scripture in which we can take heart. 1 Peter 5:7 says, "Cast all your anxiety on him because he cares for you." We have a God who cares for us. It is ridiculous to let resentment eat away at us when we have a God who cares for us and wants us to embrace a happy future with him and not a hurtful past.

91. Patience is the companion of wisdom. – Saint Augustine

We visit again the wisdom of Augustine as he talks of wisdom. They say if you want to talk with someone who knows everything, have a conversation with a teenager. Of course, when they leave the teenage years behind they realize how little they know. Experience is important to those who evaluate others. The employer likes to hire people who have a good track record of experience. Coaches like players who have experience. We assume that with experience comes more skill or wisdom. Remember the first thought in this book was about experience being the teacher in the classroom of time.

Wisdom is a very special commodity. It is not the same as knowledge. You can have knowledge and maybe score well on Jeopardy, but wisdom may not be present. Wisdom is the skill of knowing how to use knowledge well. That takes time, which takes patience, making Augustine's quote rings with truth. Young people should seek out older people with proven wisdom to mentor them.

We Americans don't do patience well. We have our fast food drive throughs and even faster food ready in the home microwave. We can stream shows on TV or record them to watch when we want to see them. We can do meetings by Zoom and cut the travel time. Patience is not something often cultivated, but God values it. Over time we learn more of what it is like to be Christlike and to apply wisdom to life. A person may know what they must do to receive salvation, but the knowledge is worthless if they don't put that knowledge in action and repent. The Parable of the Ten Virgins is evidence of this concept. All ten knew their lamps only worked when they had oil. The wise had a reserve supply and the foolish ones did not.

God desires to teach us much if we will only be patient. We get so much when we love the Lord and we learn so much when we wait on the Lord. Psalm 25:4-5 says, $_4$"Make me to know your ways, O Lord, teach me your paths. $_5$Lead me in your truth and teach me, for you are the God of my salvation, for you I wait all the day long." (ESV)

If God is teaching, he is imparting wisdom. We should also take heed to Proverbs 16:16, "How much better to get wisdom than gold, to get insight rather than silver!"

Steve Feazel

92. May God protect me from gloomy saints. – Saint Teresa of Avila

This Spanish nun was sometimes referred to as Saint Teresa of Jesus. She lived in the mid-1500s and was prominent in teaching about Christian meditation and prayer. Her writings were impactful on the church while she was alive, which was unusual during her time. She still influences other scholars centuries later. Her words above carry more humor than deep theological insight. When I first read these words, I realized that I had a kindred spirit back in the 16th century.

Gloomy saints are also usually pessimistic saints. Some people in the church today are like old fashioned cameras, they only turn out negatives. Some churches I walk into and can feel the absence of joy immediately. Usually, the building needs upkeep and there is no sense of mission or expectation that good things are going to happen. The people are like the ten spies who came back to Moses with their dismal report that the inhabitants of the land were too powerful to overcome. The Israelites rebelled at this gloom-ridden account. Even though they had the Passover and Red Sea trek miracles in their recent past, they calculated without God. That will make any saint depressed. This lack of faith cost the Israelites 40 years of wandering in the wilderness.

How many Christians today are wandering spiritually shrinking back from productive service to God because of unbelief that God will be with them and help them succeed?

I once went to an old country church that was small in numbers and seeking a new pastor. They did not have to seek a positive attitude. It was there in abundance. The grounds and building were beautifully kept and the people anticipated a bright future for their church. I could feel this positive energy the moment I walked in the foyer. How refreshing. If we, the redeemed, do not convey joy as a characteristic of our faith, do we really have any faith at all? How can anyone claim the status of Christian and not be joyful in the light of these verses: Psalm 16:11, "You make known to me the path of life; you will fill me with joy in your presence, with eternal pleasures at your right hand." And Philippians 4:4, "Rejoice in the Lord always. I will say it again: Rejoice!"

93. It is only because he became like us that we can become like him. – Dietrich Bonhoeffer

Dietrich Bonhoeffer was a German pastor, theologian and anti-Nazi dissident. His famous book is *The Cost of Discipleship*. He knew the cost well. He was arrested by the Gestapo in 1943 and executed by hanging in 1945. He was one of the most brilliant Christian minds of the mid-1900s. His words above seem so simple, but they hold deep theological implications.

As I write these comments it is the beginning of the Christmas season. Just a casual stroll through any store reveals this. We celebrate Christmas because the creator of the world, Jesus, the Son of God, came to earth in the form of a man. He took on human flesh to save the human race from eternal punishment in hell. His earthly life began in a wooden manger. Years later, he would die on a wooden cross as the Lamb of God to take away our sins, if we would only repent of those sins and accept his atonement and turn from those sins.

He then sees us as a co-heir of eternal life with him. We get to live forever in heaven with him. Bonhoeffer was right. Jesus became like us and loved us so much he gave himself for us so we can be like him and be with him forever. It just does not get any better than this.

Paul explains this truth in 1 Corinthians 15:47-49:

> 47 The first man was of the dust of the earth; the second man is of heaven. 48 As was the earthly man, so are those who are of the earth; and as is the heavenly man, so also are those who are of heaven. 49 And just as we have borne the image of the earthly man, so shall we bear the image of the heavenly man.

The first man is of course was Adam who with Eve brought about the fall of the human race. The second man, sometimes referred to as the second Adam, is Jesus who came from heaven. Adam was created by God from the earth free from sin, but chose sin. Jesus was the eternal son of God who came to earth without sin and stayed pure and free from sin so he could be the perfect offering for our sins. Because of Jesus, we can be done with sin and be like him.

94. The philosophy of the school room in one generation will be the philosophy of the government in the next. – Abraham Lincoln

It is true what a child learns in his or her formative years will become the foundation on which they will build the values that will determine the quality and success of their lives. Our 16th president knew how important this was and what vital role the public school system played. When people talk about the darkest days of America they are likely to include the start of the Civil War, Pearl Harbor or even 9-11. As I view history, I believe America's darkest day was June 25, 1962 when the Supreme Court ruled that prayer in public schools was unconstitutional. A survey revealed that 79 percent of Americans disapproved of this Court decision. This was the first serious volley by the "Separation of Church and State" crowd.

A casual student of the Constitution realizes that the doctrine of separation of church and state is not in the Constitution. The strong influence the Christian faith had on the schools is gone because of the humanist zealots and their political accessories. I went to public school from 1951 to graduation in1963. Christian values were still welcomed in the classroom. During that time I don't recall any school shootings or metal detectors at the doors and no armed guards walked the halls. Our Founders never wanted the Christian influence to be taken out of the schools. They believed it was a key ingredient of liberty and national success.

As our new nation expanded westward, schools were to be established. The Northwest Ordinance of 1787 said: "Religion, morality and knowledge being necessary to good government and the happiness of mankind, schools and the means of education shall forever be encouraged." The first two topics are gone from the schools. It is debatable if even knowledge is still given its due. Good government and happiness in the nation also seems to be waning. The Bible says in Proverbs 22:6 (NKJV), "Train up a child in the way he should go, and when he is old he will not depart from it." If you are a Christian parent you are responsible for your child learning the truth of the faith. You need to take an active role in this. We have not done a good job in this area. The humanists with their atheistic agenda are winning the day. Only 18 percent of Millennials attend church. Sacrifice and fight for your kids. Find a way for them to get the truth.

95. Few men have virtue to withstand the highest bidder. – George Washington

We now look at wisdom from another president who was the first to hold that office. When his words are reviewed, we are inclined to think they are related to those who hold political office and are tempted by corruption for self gain. I believe his words can be applied to others regardless of their occupation or pursuits in life. I think there have even been Christians who have succumbed to selling out for various benefits to self.

Let's look at the famous verse of Scripture Paul wrote to Timothy in 1 Timothy 6:10, "The love of money is the beginning of all kinds of sin. Some people have turned from the faith because of their love for money. They have made much pain for themselves because of this."

Notice, it does not say money is sinful, but the love for it is. I know people who have money, but they do not hoard it or lavish it on pleasures and things for themselves. They use it to bless other people.

The highest bidder may not come with a checkbook to win the favor of his target. Some who choose sexual encounters or valued positions of honor as more desirable than staying faithful to the faith. The virtue of steadfast faithfulness is basic to a successful Christian life. The Apostle Peter says in 1 Peter 5:8-9:

> [8]Be alert and of sober mind. Your enemy the devil prowls around like a roaring lion looking for someone to devour. [9]Resist him, standing firm in the faith, because you know that the family of believers throughout the world is undergoing the same kind of sufferings.

101 Thoughts for a Better Life

Peter is writing to believers. He is warning them that Satan has not given up on getting them back in his control. He describes the devil as a hungry lion looking to devour even Christians. Peter says to resist him and stand firm. To do this you must be in a state of total surrender to Jesus Christ with his Holy Spirit well established in your heart. You must spend time in Bible study and prayer to stay in spiritual shape to win the spiritual warfare with Satan. In so doing, the highest bidder, who is the agent of Satan, will not dent your steadfast faith in Jesus Christ.

96. The spirit of envy can destroy; it can never build. – Margaret Thatcher

When Margaret Thatcher was the prime minister of Great Britain was known as the "Iron Lady" because of her uncompromising principles. Her above words seem more likely to come from a theologian or pastor than the head of a prominent world nation. Envy is being unhappy because of someone else's good fortune. Sometimes envy can be so extreme it can become pathological and can be considered a delusional disorder.

Envy emerged early in the Scriptures and resulted in the first murder when Cain killed his brother Able. The brothers of Joseph who sold him into slavery and Saul's animosity toward David are examples. However, envy can exist even when the person one is envying doesn't know it. A person can have envy toward a whole group of people who are perceived to have better circumstance and fortune in life.

Some people have gained good fortune at no effort on their part. They may have inherited wealth or property. They may have won it by legal gambling. They may have been promoted to a lucrative position by an act of favoritism when they were undeserving of it. No matter who or what group one directs envy towards, the result is the one doing the envying is suffering the greatest harm. Envy is like the twin sibling of jealousy. Both are destructive to a Christian's spiritual life.

As the Iron Lady said, "envy destroys." It cannot build because it is deeply rooted in self-centeredness. You cannot envy and trust in God at the same time. Envy puts self on the throne of the heart. So much time is spent focusing on others and what they have that one does not put the required effort needed to make achievements possible. Envy is focusing on others and not on Jesus Christ.

Proverbs 23:17 puts in bluntly and accurately, "Do not let your heart envy sinners, but always be zealous for the fear of the Lord."

97. We make a living by what we get, but we make a life by what we give. –Winston Churchill

Winston Churchill was a giant figure during World War II. His determination for victory inspired the British people as they endured the German air raids. He stood strong during a very tough time. He was both practical and insightful. He was a man of wisdom and his above words verify this.

Yes, we do make a living by what we get and God does not begrudge this. We need to be about "getting" because as adults we need to make an income to support the family and provide opportunities for children to learn and thrive in life. Getting is not a bad thing unless it becomes the only thing. We need to make a living, but we also need to make a life. This is important for the Christian.

The key characteristic of a Christian is love and love cares for the good of others. We are to make a life that counts by giving. The first place where giving should start is with yourself. If you want abundant life, you start by giving yourself to Jesus Christ as you surrender your all to him and accept him as your savior. This action ends the selfish self and allows you the freedom to give in other ways.

Giving does not always have to be in money. When I got involved in writing and learned more about how publishing worked in the three areas of traditional, hybrids, and self-publishing, I learned much through the hard-knocks classroom. Friends have come to me asking for advice and hands-on help to get their books self-published. It has been a joy to freely provide help to them in this area and save them money and the agony the process of publishing can sometimes bring.

I have looked to my past and realized I have been a recipient of gifts from others. My parents, friends and my wife who is my first line editor have all given to me. It is only natural that I pay forward and give to others. And, since Jesus gave his life for me, it is imperative I give to others in his name. That does create a life that counts. We need to live the words found in 2 Corinthians 9:6-7:

> 6 Remember this: Whoever sows sparingly will also reap sparingly, and whoever sows generously will also reap generously. 7 Each of you should give what you have decided in your heart to give, not reluctantly or under compulsion, for God loves a cheerful giver."

98. Surely the principles of Christianity lead to action as well as meditation. –William Wilberforce

William Wilberforce is a bright star in the sky of history. He was a Member of Parliament in the late 1700s and early 1800s. He carried the burden to end the slave trade. It was frustrating work. He brought it before Parliament only to be denied for some 20 years. It got so frustrating for him that he once wanted to quit Parliament and become a pastor. The captain of a slave ship, John Newton, who was converted, became a minister and wrote the song *Amazing Grace*, told Wilberforce to stay in Parliament and keep with the cause.

In 1807 Wilberforce was successful in ending this atrocious practice of the slave trade. Before his death, he was able to see slavery in the British Empire totally abolished. William Wilberforce knew what it meant to put Christianity into action and not just make it a meditation experience. His efforts helped to put an end to slavery without the bloodshed that was experienced in America for the same end.

My wife and I happily support Samaritan's Purse, the disaster relief organization headed by Franklin Graham of the Billy Graham Evangelistic Association. This organization puts Christianity into action. Writing a check is easy. We also put Christianity in action as we both mentor young Christians who seek a deep relationship with Jesus and discover their ministry in God's kingdom.

In the history of the Christian faith, monks and nuns have withdrawn from the world to seek a disciplined spiritual life. I don't criticize those for doing so if they are convinced this was or is God's will for their lives. Great achievements that have come forth from monasteries and convents, but I feel the great need today is for more Christians to put their faith in action. Pew meditation needs to be secondary to culture penetration by believers. James 1:22-24 provides us with needed wisdom:

> $_{22}$ Do not merely listen to the word, and so deceive yourselves. Do what it says. $_{23}$ Anyone who listens to the word but does not do what it says is like someone who looks at his face in a mirror $_{24}$ and, after looking at himself, goes away and immediately forgets what he looks like.

99. There is no short cut to achievement. – George Washington Carver

George Washington Carver was born during the Civil War and died during World War II. He was one of the most prominent black scientists of the early 20th century. He introduced the practice rotating crops from year to year to prevent soil depletion. I see this taking place personally as I view the farm field from my front porch. One year it's corn; the next year it's soybeans. You can be assured that the success Carver experienced was not rapidly obtained. There are no short cuts in scientific experiments. In farming, you don't plant one week, then harvest the next.

The words of George Washington Carver have proven true in my life. After I was called to be a minister, it took ten years before I was pastoring my own church. Many years of education had to take place. When I got the dream of being a writer and thus expanding my ministry through the page, it was 14 years later before my first book was published. When I see college football players selected on draft day by an NFL team assuring them of becoming millionaires, I know they have put in countless hours of practice, and conditioning to hone their skills to merit this fantastic opportunity.

We have many today who don't believe they have to pay the dues. They are the "right now" generation and they expect top shelf experiences immediately if not sooner. Young people need to realize they don't have microwave lives. Worthy achievements take hard work and time. Some people are constantly looking to get rich quick. They flit from one shiny thing to another with disappointment being their reward. They would do better focusing on one thing and doing it better as time goes on until they experience great achievement.

The Christian life is a journey. You don't reach maturity and leadership status overnight. It takes time, learning and practice. Jesus spent three years with his disciples. Timothy and Titus were mentored for years by Paul. Be determined to be committed to put in the time and effort to be the best servant of Jesus Christ you can be and you will be amazed at what you achieve, and may it all be for his glory. Proverbs 6:9-11 tells us that achievement does not come to the lazy:

> $_9$ How long will you lie there, you sluggard? When will you get up from your sleep? $_{10}$ A little sleep, a little slumber, a little folding of the hands to rest— $_{11}$ and poverty will come on you like a thief and scarcity like an armed man.

100. Once we recognize our need for Jesus, then the building of our faith begins. It is a daily, moment-by-moment life of absolute dependence upon Him for everything. – Catherine Marshall

As the widow of the famed Chaplain of the Senate, Peter Marshall, Catherine Marshall touched the lives of millions through her more than 60 books. The phrase in her above quote is a true description of the Christian life: "It is a daily moment-by-moment life of absolute dependence upon Him for everything."

She reveals to us that living the Christian life is not a part time venture. We would do well from time to time to take spiritual inventory of our lives and ask ourselves if we are living life with "absolute dependence upon Jesus for everything." We have our moments where we want to say, "I got this." But, when it comes to living the Christian life, we need to be saying, "Lord, you got me."

The two people in the Bible who are outstanding examples of this type of faith commitment are Joseph of the Old Testament and Paul in the New Testament. Joseph had many unjust things happen to him, but his faith in his God never wavered. He went from slave to number two in command in the great kingdom of Egypt. Paul came became the 12th Apostle as an outsider, chosen by Christ to have that role. He faced many trials from enemies of the faith and those who claimed to be of the faith which opposed him. He never lost his dependency on and his trust in Christ.

If the people in the Sunday morning pews took the above words of Catherine Marshall seriously, the Christian faith in America would be revolutionized and the secular culture gripping our land would be changed. Marshall is telling us that practicing the presence of Jesus Christ is important for living a successful Christian life. She is right in stride with Jesus saying that we must take up our cross daily if we want to be his disciples. Luke 9:23 has his words, Then he said to them all: "Whoever wants to be my disciple must deny themselves and take up their cross daily and follow me."

The Christian life is definitely not a part time thing. You are all in or not in at all.

Steve Feazel

101. In my Father's house are many rooms; if it were not so, I would have told you. I am going there to prepare a place for you. – Jesus (John 14:2)

You must realize that God the Father gave Jesus his Son the responsibility of creating the world. John1:1-3 states:

> $_1$In the beginning was the Word, and the Word was with God, and the Word was God. $_2$ He was with God in the beginning. $_3$Through him all things were made; without him nothing was made that has been made.

"Through him all things were made." This would include man. It is therefore mind-blowing to think that the Jesus who created man, us, was the one who took on human flesh and died for us so our sins could be forgiven and qualify us for heaven. This creator made all the animals including the platypus that is a mammal with a duck bill and lays eggs. Who says Jesus didn't have a sense of humor? He also made all the beauty in nature that we marvel at as we look upon it.

The fantastic thing is He's not finished creating. He is in heaven with his Father, but he is working at making a place for us. He's building us a room in his Father's house. It's incredible to think the Creator of the world has made himself a private contractor for our eternal dwelling. There is not a pleasure, an honor or any amount of money in this world that can compare with what Jesus is doing for us in his father's house.

We need to be inspired to lead others to Christ so Jesus will have to make more additions. My favorite singing group which were active in the 1970s and 1980s, The 2nd Chapter of Acts, had a song entitled, *Mansion Builder*. It contained the lyrical line, "Why should I worry? Why should I fret? Because, I have a Mansion Builder who ain't through with me yet."

Jesus will definitely build a room for you in his Father's house if you first make room for him in your heart. When you do this a reservation is made for that special room. Whenever you experience a disappointment or heartache in this life, remember the room being made for you. It's there in your future and it will be awesome, and you're going to love the neighbors.

Let us take heart in the following words in Revelation 21:1-4:

> ₁Then I saw "a new heaven and a new earth," for the first heaven and the first earth had passed away, and there was no longer any sea. ₂I saw the Holy City, the New Jerusalem, coming down out of heaven from God, prepared as a bride beautifully dressed for her husband. ₃And I heard a loud voice from the throne saying, "Look! God's dwelling place is now among the people, and he will dwell with them. They will be his people, and God himself will be with them and be their God. ₄He will wipe every tear from their eyes. There will be no more death or mourning or crying or pain, for the old order of things has passed away."

Please, don't miss out on this!

Final Words

Paul writes in Romans 8:31 "What, then, shall we say in response to these things? If God is for us, who can be against us?" God is 100 percent on our side, so it makes sense to believe his Word and trust him for everything all the time. I hope some of these thoughts helped you in your spiritual journey. If you have not accepted Jesus Christ as your savior, I invite you to do so by praying the sinner's prayer below. As I reviewed all of these 101 thoughts I leave six take-a-ways:
- Jesus does not guarantee prosperity assuring us health and wealth, he promises his presence
- Lukewarmness is the number one problem in American churches today
- It all comes down to who will control your life, Jesus or self
- We need to live life with eternity in focus
- True discipleship with Christlike character is not the exception, its expected
- Don't calculate without God

You may have your own. I would love to hear from you as to what they might be. Please feel free to email them to me at my email address at the bottom of the next page.

Steve Feazel

Sinner's Prayer

Dear God, I know that I'm a sinner, and there's nothing I can do to save myself. But because of the resurrection of Jesus Christ, I can be saved. I confess my complete helplessness to forgive my own sin. At this moment, I trust Christ alone as the One who bore my sin when He died on the cross. He did all that will ever be necessary for me to stand in Your holy presence. Jesus is Lord and the gift of God. Because of Your grace, I'm born again. I'm grateful that You've promised to receive me despite my many sins and failures. Father, I take You at Your word. I thank You that You're my Savior. Thank You for the assurance that You'll walk with me through the deep valley. In Jesus' name. Amen.

If you prayed this prayer, please let me know through the below email.

stevefeazel@gmail.com

Index

The 101 Thoughts' numbers are listed under various topics so the reader may refer to a topic of interest and know what Thoughts are related to that topic.

Character
1, 2, 3, 4, 5, 6, 7, 16, 17, 18,20, 22,23,24,26, 30, 34, 35, 36, 40, 44, 51, 58, 61, 62, 63, 64, 65, 67, 68, 70,73, 76, 77, 79, 81, 86, 87, 89, 90,91, 96

Christian Living
1, 4, 5, 7, 9, 11, 12, 13, 17, 22, 25, 28, 33, 36, 46, 48, 49, 50, 53, 54, 56, 57, 60, 72, 78, 89, 94, 99

Christian Love
31, 32, 66, 76

Discipleship
8, 11, 13, 16, 24, 27, 29, 34, 42, 52, 55, 61, 66, 67, 69, 80, 84, 98

Holy Spirit
7, 18, 19, 39

Jesus – Faith
2, 3, 10, 14, 21, 25, 27, 31, 38, 39, 45, 64, 66, 71, 74, 75, 82, 83, 88, 92, 93, 100, 101

Lukewarmness
9, 41, 42, 51, 53, 62, 66, 69, 80, 85

Money – Stewardship
3, 6, 8, 15, 37, 41, 47, 68, 74, 77, 95, 97

Other Books by Steve Feazel

The Three Cs that Made America Great: Christianity, Capitalism and the Constitution.
Coauthor with Mike Huckabee, Foreword by Sean Hannity

America in the Balance: The American Dream vs The Woke Nightmare
Coauthored with Rick Scarborough, Foreword by Mike Huckabee

Voting Christian Values: Reclaiming Our Moral Heritage
How to vote your faith, Foreword by Mike Huckabee

Lose the Weight and Keep the Faith
Coauthored with Nick Gaglione – Getting fit for Christ

Abduction: How Liberalism Steals Our Children's Hearts and Mind
Coauthored with Dr. Carol Swain, Foreword by Tony Perkins

CPR for Believers: Principles for a Quality Life
Christian Inspiration for victorious living

The Clock and the Prophecy
Novel for middle grade school students through adults

The Faith and the Life
A full discipleship course working as a topical Bible study

Basic 7: A Discipleship Course for New Christians
Seven short lessons on essential truths of the Christian faith

Secession
Novel – suspense/thriller – socialism vs capitalism in America

The Lost Letter
Novel – suspense/thriller – a couple cope with danger seeking a Pauline epistle - Coming in 2024

Meeting God's Conditions for Revival: An In Depth Study of 2 Chronicles 7:14 Coming 2024

About the Author

Steve Feazel is an ordained minister in an evangelical denomination. He served as pastor and taught as an adjunct professor of business at various universities. He produced three award-winning, faith-based documentaries on social issues including the pro-life side of abortion. Besides holding a degree from seminary, he has an MBA from Arizona State University. Steve's first published book entitled, *Abduction: How Liberalism Steals Our Children's Hearts and Minds*, was coauthored with Dr. Carol Swain. He also coauthored a book with Mike Huckabee, *The Three Cs that Made America Great: Christianity, Capitalism, and the Constitution*. Steve has written novels and Christian inspiration books which can be discovered on his website along with other ministries in which he is involved. Steve and his wife Edy live near Mount Vernon, Ohio. They have two grown sons and five grandchildren.

Steve is available for speaking engagements and seminars.

His personal website is **visionword.com**.

Email: stevefeazel@gmail.com

Made in the USA
Columbia, SC
04 April 2024